The Ukrainian Night

The
Ukrainian
Night

An Intimate History of Revolution

Marci Shore

Yale UNIVERSITY PRESS

New Haven & London

Published with assistance from the Kingsley Trust Association Publication
Fund established by the Scroll and Key Society of Yale College

Yale University Press books may be purchased in quantity for educational,
business, or promotional use. For information, please e-mail
sales.press@yale.edu (U.S. office) or sales@yaleup.co.uk (U.K. office).

Set in Janson type by Integrated Publishing Solutions.
Printed in the United States of America.

Library of Congress Control Number: 2017941041
ISBN 978-0-300-21868-8 (hardcover : alk. paper)

A catalogue record for this book is available from the British Library.

This paper meets the requirements of ANSI/NISO Z39.48-1992
(Permanence of Paper).

10 9 8 7 6 5 4 3 2 1

Kalewkowi i Talijce, in hope of a better world to come

Знаете ли вы
        украинскую ночь?
Нет,
     вы не знаете украинской ночи!
Здесь
   небо
      от дыма
         становится
            черно . . .

Do you know
        the Ukrainian night?
No,
     you do not know the Ukrainian night!
Here
   the sky
      turns black
         from smoke . . .

—Vladimir Mayakovsky, "Долг Украине" (Debt to Ukraine), 1926

Contents

Preface   xiii
Map of Ukraine   xviii
Map of Central Kiev   xix
Note on Transliteration   xxi

PART 1 Revolution, the Maidan

The Sky Turns Black from Smoke   3
The Land of Gogol   5
The Grandeur of Its Intentions   7
Fantasies of Galicia   14
The Revolutions That Were Not   24
"Likes" Don't Count   29
Fathers and Sons   37
Self-Organization   43
The Bell Tower   46
Noah's Ark   51

Contents

"It was my choice" 57

When Time Was Smashed 65

Automaidan 73

Values 79

The Very Atmosphere Had Some Qualities 85

The Nonanalytical Point 90

The Buses from Lviv 101

Corpses 103

The Solidarity of the Shaken 105

Burning Flesh 110

"You will all be dead" 113

Pornographic Portraits 119

The Revolutionary Soul 122

Dialectics of Transparency 126

Chekhov's Gun 129

PART 2 War, East of Kiev

Russian Tourists 133

Caligula at the Gates 136

Grandma at War 140

Nothing Is True (The Surrealism of Ostriches) 142

Putin's Sirens 149

Zhidobandera on the Dnipro 159

Smart Kids Like You 163

"We understood perfectly ..." 167

The Volunteer Movement 177

The Specter of Communism 183

A Civilizational Choice 186

Black Lizard on Red Square 190

Free Hugs for Patriots 197

Divided Families 202

Alchevsk 205

Contents

Zombies in the Donbas   208

The Time Is Out of Joint   212

World Order   221

Goodbye, Lenin   223

Cicero's Rome   229

Do We Know the Ukrainian Night?   236

"We cannot be bought"   238

Theater of the Absurd   244

Dostoevsky's Demons   247

"At the end of the day this soldier feels sorry"   250

Ice Skating Lessons   261

There Is No Absolute   264

Everything Is Possible   267

Dictionary of Translatable and Untranslatable Words   271

Notes   273

Acknowledgments   287

Preface

The Ukrainian revolution of 2013–2014 on the Maidan was the most extraordinary thing I have seen in the quarter century I have been coming to Eastern Europe. The political became the existential. I saw friends and colleagues I had known for years making decisions they would have found unimaginable a few months earlier. People who valued their privacy suddenly laid bare their souls. Though I eventually made several trips to Lviv, Kiev, and Dnipropetrovsk (renamed Dnipro in May 2016), I watched the Maidan mainly from Vienna, where I was living that year. Being close enough to Kiev to see Ukrainian friends who were traveling back and forth, and at the same time immersed in the media culture of the West, I felt how little this revolution was understood. Journalists and politicians commented on

NATO policy, oil pipelines, and international finance, but not on the transformation of human souls.

Early in the twentieth century the Polish philosopher Stanisław Brzozowski wrote, "What is not biography—is nothing at all." This is my point of departure. This book began as a more modest essay, a portrait of the Ukrainian literary translator Jurko Prochasko. The original title was "'It was My Choice': A Phenomenology of the Ukrainian Revolution." This phenomenology was in the spirit of Edmund Husserl's philosophy: a description of revolution as pure subjective experience. This book is not an analysis of contemporary politics in Ukraine; I make no arguments or predictions about political outcomes. This is an exploration of revolution as a lived experience given to individuals.

I try in the pages that follow to understand what pushed some of my own friends and colleagues—people like myself, like ourselves—to places where they had never expected to find themselves, what pushed them towards a willingness to risk their lives. All of them experienced a moment when it was imperative to make a choice. This was "choosing" in the strongest, existentialist sense described by Jean-Paul Sartre: "Life is nothing until it is lived; but it is yours to make sense of, and the value of it is nothing else but the sense that you choose." Time and time again I heard, in different languages, "*it was my choice.*"

"Dostoevsky once wrote," Sartre goes on to say, "'If God did not exist, everything would be permitted'; and that, for existentialism, is the starting point. Everything is indeed permitted if God does not exist, and man is in consequence forlorn, for he cannot find anything to depend upon either within or outside himself." Sartre tried to move man in the place vacated by God; Marx tried to move History there. The Soviet Union—the materialization of Marxist metaphysics—was modern man's most audacious attempt to replace God. Its failure, and more broadly the failure of Marxism, the last of the grand narratives, arguably brought about the end of modernity as such.

Postmodernity began with the relinquishing of attempts to replace God: now not only was God dead, but moreover there was no one and nothing to take His place. The fate of truth in such a world was not so clear. Nearly a quarter century after the fall of communism, the Ukrainian revolution illuminated anew the border between modernity and postmodernity. It also raised questions about what would come next. "With the revolution of 2014, the postmodern ended in Ukraine," wrote the Russian historian Ilya Gerasimov. "We still do not know how to conceptualize this new reality."

The Ukrainian revolution on Kiev's Maidan, though bound up with a particular history, simultaneously laid bare universal questions about the nature of selfhood, the plasticity of temporality, and the fate of truth. When does a protest cross an invisible boundary to become a revolution? What brings parents and children together, and what splits generations apart? Under what circumstances does fear disappear? How is revolutionary time different from the time of *byt*, the untranslatable Russian word for the heaviness of everyday life? How are the experiences of time and space altered? Why does the distinction between night and day fade? How is selfhood both realized and overcome by solidarity? What does it mean for people to film themselves being shot? What conditions allow the boundary between reality and fiction to be effaced?

The second part of this book, about the aftermath of the Maidan and the war in the Donbas, explores in particular this last question. When the Iron Curtain fell in 1989, Francis Fukuyama declared "the End of History": the eighteenth century Enlightenment, celebrating its faith in reason and truth, had conceived a teleology of progress that seemingly concluded in liberal democracy. So it is perhaps fitting that the end of "the End of History" be brought about by a discomposing fusion of Romantic will and "post-factuality."

In this world after the End of History, both American capitalism and post-Soviet oligarchy have produced a specialty PR market for gangsters; and reality television has done away with the distinction between the fictional and the real. This is a world where warlords can promote themselves on Instagram and Twitter, and Ukrainian and American oligarchs with presidential aspirations can share a strategic advisor.

Karl Marx was untimely when he wrote, "all that is solid melts into air." In the mid-nineteenth century, the observation was still premature. Perhaps this is no longer the case: in a "post-factual" world, much that seemed solid has melted into air. Yet people remain. This is a work of nonfiction, a history of a revolution as it was experienced by those who chose to take part in it. The purpose of writing history is like that of writing literature: to allow the reader an encounter with alterity, an imaginative leap into another time and place, a possibility of understanding the Other. In this sense, I hope that the chapters of this book about the war in the Donbas can play some small role in providing a human face to yet another tragedy of the kind Neville Chamberlain described as a "quarrel in a faraway country between people of whom we know nothing."

New Haven
January 2017

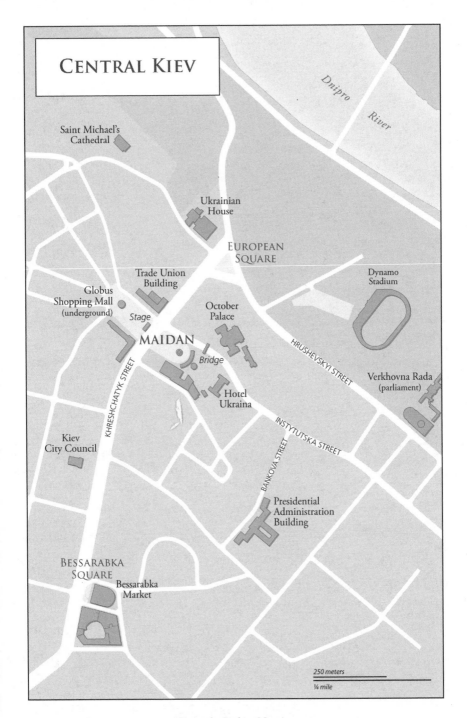

CENTRAL KIEV

Saint Michael's
Cathedral

Ukrainian
House

EUROPEAN
SQUARE

Dynamo
Stadium

Trade Union
Building

Globus
Shopping Mall
(underground)

Stage

October
Palace

MAIDAN

Bridge

Hotel
Ukraina

Kiev
City Council

KHRESHCHATYK STREET

HRUSHEVSKYI STREET

INSTYTUTSKA STREET

BANKOVA STREET

Verkhovna Rada
(parliament)

Presidential
Administration
Building

BESSARABKA
SQUARE

Bessarabka
Market

Dnipro River

250 meters

¼ mile

© 2017 by Beehive Mapping

Note on Transliteration

Ukraine is a bilingual country. Ukrainian, the official state language, tends to be dominant in western Ukraine; Russian tends to be dominant in eastern Ukraine. Polish, especially but not exclusively in western Ukraine, is fairly common as well—a century ago this was also true of Yiddish and German. These generalizations obscure, though, the everyday reality of casual bilingualism. It is normal for conversations to occur in two languages, or for journalists to conduct an interview in one language while the person being interviewed responds in another. In Ukraine I spoke Russian and Polish and English, occasionally German. In the case of the novelist Serhiy Zhadan, for instance, I spoke to him in Polish about a novel he had written in Ukrainian and I had read in English. He spoke to me in Russian. This situation was very Ukrainian.

This multilingualism—enriching for Ukraine itself—inevitably causes difficulties for transliteration from Cyrillic to Latin alphabets. Most Ukrainians use more than one version of their names—a Ukrainian version, perhaps a different Russian version, and a medley of diminutives. For example: "Ihor" in Ukrainian becomes "Igor" in Russian, "Yevhen" becomes "Yevgen," "Mykhailo" becomes "Mikhail," "Oleksiy" becomes "Aleksei," "Oleksandr" becomes "Aleksandr." Further, "Yevhenii" or "Yevhen" or "Yevgen" becomes "Zhenia" in diminutive form, "Mikhail" or "Mykhailo" becomes "Misha," "Kateryna" becomes "Katia," both "Aleksandr" and "Aleksandra" become "Sasha," while "Oleksandr" becomes "Oles." The Library of Congress has one English transliteration system for Russian and another for Ukrainian (written in the Cyrillic alphabet, like Russian, but using a small number of different letters). Both languages transliterate differently into German and Polish than they do into English ("Juri" or "Jurij Andruchowytsch" in German, "Jurij Andruchowycz" in Polish, "Iurii" or "Yuri" or "Yurii Andrukhovych" in English). This is a book about individuals, most of whom—in an age of an internet dominated by the Latin alphabet—have already chosen for themselves a Latinized spelling of their names. And so I defer to the choices made by the book's protagonists ("Jurko Prochasko" rather than "Iurko Prokhas'ko," "Victoria Narizhna" rather than "Viktoria"). Most often I refer to people as I myself addressed them, making exceptions for clarity when names overlap ("Yevhenii Monastyrskyi" rather than "Zhenia" due to multiple

"Zhenias," "Katia Mischchenko" and "Kateryna Iakovlenko" due to multiple "Katias," "Ihor Petrovsky" and "Igor Shchupak," "Oleh Repan" and "Oleg Marchuk").

In referring to names of places in Ukraine, I transliterate from Ukrainian ("Luhansk" rather than "Lugansk") following the Library of Congress system, yet modifying to avoid diacritical marks. I make an exception in cases where a Russian transliteration has effectively become anglicized and already familiar to English-language readers (and so, following the *New York Times*, "Kiev" rather than "Kyiv," "Odessa" rather than "Odesa").

None of this is meant as an intervention in language politics. My hope is to avoid gratuitously confusing non-Slavic-speaking readers, and to respect the personal (not necessarily political, perhaps more often aesthetic) choices of this book's protagonists. These are, of course, imperfect solutions to problems for which there are no perfect solutions.

PART I

Revolution, the Maidan

The Sky Turns Black from Smoke

Close to midnight on Tuesday, 18 February 2014, twenty-one-year-old Misha Martynenko, reeking of smoke, returned to the Kiev apartment he shared with his mother, his grandmother, and his ten-year-old sister. He was wearing a white beaded cross around his neck. In his mother's face Misha saw that she had aged several years since they had parted that morning. He looked in the mirror: his own face was the color of pallid charcoal. His eyes were bulging. He began to cry.

Nearly ten hours later Misha awoke still wearing clothing covered with soot and dirt. The city was the same color: that day the sky in Kiev turned black from smoke. On the streets surrounding the central square known as the Maidan, thousands of people were digging up bricks and paving stones to build barricades. They set fire to clothing and tires and anything else that

3

could burn. They were defending themselves against the *Berku-tovtsy*, the Ukrainian government's specially trained riot police, storm troopers with gas masks whose eyes it was impossible to see. Their silver shields covered their faces and torsos, creating a moving bunker not easily penetrated by the Molotov cocktails. Far above the flaming barricades, on the rooftop of the high-rise Hotel Ukraina, snipers fired downwards, and bodies fell, corpses amidst black smoke.

One of those shot in the neck by a sniper was a paramedic named Olesia Zhukovska, who was wearing a white uniform with a red cross. She was exactly Misha's age. As blood poured from her neck, she typed on her phone the Twitter message: "I am dying."

The Land of Gogol

On Wednesday evening, 19 February 2014, the political scientist and prominent Ukrainian intellectual Mykola Riabchuk lectured to a crowded room in Vienna. Mykola spoke calmly, reflectively. Although he was not optimistic, he was hopeful. He had no doubts that the fight for freedom in Ukraine would continue. Perhaps this time the fight would not succeed; but Mykola was certain that, if not this time, then some day it would. He answered all questions undefensively. He said nothing to the audience of the fact that his wife and their twenty-six-year-old son were in Kiev, that his son, Yuri, had returned home at 4 that morning and was now on the Maidan once again, that Mykola did not know whether or not Yuri would be killed there that night, perhaps right now as he was speaking here in the library of the Institute for Human Sciences.

(His parents never asked him to stay home, Yuri told me when we met later in Kiev. "You cross a line . . . ," he said.

"Did you think you could get killed?" I asked.

"Yeah, I did.")

"What can we do?" asked a young Polish woman in the audience.

In response Mykola described a scene from Nikolai Gogol's play *The Inspector-General*. At the end of the play a country squire named Piotr Ivanovich Bobchinsky approached the Inspector General from the capital of Saint Petersburg with a "humble request": he begged his Excellency most worshipfully, when he returned to Saint Petersburg, to tell the tsar that there was a man called Piotr Ivanovich Bobchinsky who lived in this town. To simply remember that there was a man called Piotr Ivanovich Bobchinsky.

"Just remember," Mykola answered the young woman, "that there is a country called Ukraine."

The Grandeur of Its Intentions

"The first represents the exaltation of the executioner by the executioner," wrote the French philosopher Albert Camus, describing the difference between Nazism and Bolshevism, "the second, more dramatic in concept, the exaltation of the executioner by the victims. The former never dreamed of liberating all men, but only of liberating a few by subjugating the rest. The latter, in its most profound principle, aims at liberating all men by provisionally enslaving them all. It must be granted the grandeur of its intentions."

Twenty-first century Ukraine was heir to the grandeur of these intentions, to daring experiments. "Both Europe and Russia conduct research in our laboratory," wrote the Ukrainian novelist Taras Prochasko. "They experiment, although they have no idea what the result of the synthesis might be."

The experiments began long before the Bolshevik Revolution. For centuries the lands of today's Ukraine were ruled from Vilnius or Warsaw. In the early modern period, these lands were divided between the Polish-Lithuanian Commonwealth and the tsarist Russian empire. When in the eighteenth century the Commonwealth was partitioned by its imperial neighbors, Lviv and much of what is now western Ukraine was taken by Habsburg Empress Maria Theresa. Present-day Lviv, previously Polish Lwów, became Austrian Lemberg, the object of the Habsburg empire's "civilizing mission."

The First World War brought the old imperial Europe to an end. Early in 1917, bread shortages in frozen Petrograd led to demonstrations, strikes, and mutiny by Tsar Nicholas II's troops. An empire fell. The tsar abdicated his throne. A precarious "Dual Power" took his place: fragile authority divided between a liberal Provisional Government and a socialist Petrograd Soviet. As the war against Germany and Austria wore on, disillusioned peasants began to protest. The Provisional Government convened a militia in the countryside; peasants seized land and refused to deliver grain. In the cities there were food shortages. Disenchantment radicalized the peasantry.

In April 1917 Lenin arrived in Petrograd—where, in his own words, he "found power lying in the streets and simply picked it up." In the midst of anarchy, the Bolsheviks made a radical choice. When in October 1917 Lenin and the Bolsheviks stormed the Winter Palace, they acted on behalf of a metaphysical proletariat—one yet to come into being.

Shortly thereafter, Ukrainian leaders in Kiev declared a Ukrainian National Republic. Galician Ukrainian leaders hesitated to join them; most then still wanted an autonomous Ukrainian crown land within the Habsburg empire. Soon, though, this became impossible: the Habsburg empire itself was no more. On 1 November 1918 the Ukrainian National Council declared a West Ukrainian People's Republic, with Lviv as its capital; a week later Poland declared independence. Through most of November Polish and Ukrainian forces fought for Lviv in a battle that concluded with a Polish victory—and a Polish pogrom against Jews. Habsburg Lemberg, briefly Ukrainian Lviv, was now again Polish Lwów.

In March 1918, believing that the worldwide revolution would begin momentarily, Lenin negotiated a separate peace with the Germans. Yet in the lands of what had been the Russian Empire, the war did not end in 1918 at all; it bled into a gruesome civil war between the Bolsheviks and their assorted enemies, as well as between the Bolsheviks and newly independent Poland, created from disparate pieces of the German, Habsburg, and tsarist empires. Everywhere people fled violence and pogroms; the lands between Warsaw and Petersburg filled with refugees. Kiev, divided like Paris into a Left and Right Bank, was a large metropolis; even so, under the pressure of refugees, "the City swelled, expanded, overflowed like leavened dough rising out of its baking tin," as Mikhail Bulgakov described in *White Guard*. By the time it was all over, Kiev had been occupied by five different armies. And four European empires had fallen: German, Ottoman, Habsburg, and tsarist Russian. Galicia and western Volhynia—present-day western Ukraine—belonged to newly independent Poland; Kiev, Kharkiv, Dnipropetrovsk, Odessa, Donetsk, and Luhansk—cities of present-day central and eastern Ukraine—were controlled by the Red Army.

In 1922, Lenin declared the formation of the Soviet Union, with the Ukrainian Soviet Socialist Republic as one of its founding constituent republics. Two years later, Lenin died. When Stalin came to power at the end of that decade, he ordered the collectivization of agriculture. With all means possible and impossible, Ukrainian peasants resisted the confiscation of their property and their land. Collectivization was bloody and savage; its effect on agricultural productivity was disastrous. After Stalin in 1932 raised Ukraine's grain procurement quotas by 44 percent, the peasants could no longer feed themselves: Soviet law required that no grain be distributed to collective farm members until Moscow had received its share. Party officials, aided by regular troops and secret police units, waged a war against peasants who refused to give up their grain. The result of a poor harvest and draconian quotas was mass death. As Stalin forcibly requisitioned their grain, selling it abroad and using the hard currency to fund industrialization, Ukrainian peasants became emaciated, then swollen. Some resorted to cannibalism. In Soviet Ukraine between 1932 and 1934 more than three and a half million people died of starvation.

Then came the Stalinist Terror. Stalin declared that just as the socialist victory was assured, the class struggle paradoxically intensified. The enemy, ever more desperate, concealed himself: now he could be anywhere, including in one's own bed. Constant vigilance was a necessity; no one was to be trusted. "Enemies of the people" lurked everywhere. They were plotters of counterrevolution; they were wreckers and saboteurs; they were capitalists and imperialists, nationalist conspirators and Trotskyite spies. Stalin had always blamed Ukrainians themselves for the famine; now this accusation took the fantastical form of an imaginary plot. It was the time of the Great Terror: mass arrests, confessions extracted by torture, hundreds of thousands of executions. In 1937 and 1938 the NKVD, the Soviet secret police, recorded 123,421 executions in Soviet Ukraine.

On 1 September 1939 Nazi Germany attacked Poland. German soldiers appeared briefly in Lwów, yet quickly—as agreed by Hitler and Stalin in the August 1939 Molotov-Ribbentrop Pact—the city was taken by Stalin's Red Army and integrated into Soviet Ukraine. The Red Army, it claimed, had come to liberate Jews and Ukrainians from Polish oppression. Once the Habsburgs had played the Poles against the Ukrainians; now the Soviets played the Ukrainians against the Poles. Refugees from German-occupied Poland poured into baroque, once Habsburg Lviv, together with Stalinist terror.

"They liberated us and there's nothing to be done for it," regretted Ukrainian composer Stanyslav Lyudkevych.

This was not the Ukraine the Ukrainians had wanted.

When on 22 June 1941 Hitler attacked the Soviet Union, many Ukrainians welcomed the appearance of the Germans as an end to Soviet terror. In eastern Galicia, German soldiers arrived with Ukrainian auxiliaries, many of them members of the Organization of Ukrainian Nationalists faction led by Stepan Bandera. As the Wehrmacht moved eastward in late June and early July 1941, Soviet NKVD officers made mass arrests—and in Lviv massacred thousands of their prisoners. German and Ukrainian nationalist propaganda both blamed the massacre on "Judeo-Bolsheviks" and called for revenge. Jews were forced to collect the corpses of the murdered prisoners. On 30 June 1941 Stepan Bandera's fellow nationalist leader Yaroslav Stetsko proclaimed a Ukrainian state. A day later saw the climax of a Ukrainian pogrom against Jews. Germans filmed the pogrom; Ukrainians carried it out.

Ukrainian nationalists had hoped for autonomy under the Germans; they were disappointed. Shortly after the proclamation of Ukrainian statehood, the Germans arrested both Stetsko and Bandera. They also forced Jews into the ghetto. The Ukrainian Insurgent Army, associated with the Organization of Ukrainian Nationalists, carried out a gruesome ethnic cleansing of Poles in German-occupied former eastern Poland. By July 1943 Lviv was *Judenrein*. The following summer—on 23 July

1944—the Polish Home Army, anti-German Polish partisans loyal to the Polish government-in-exile, took partial control of Lviv, and fought Ukrainian nationalists. Four days later, the Red Army occupied the city center.

As the war came to an end, both Soviets and Ukrainian locals in eastern Galicia agreed on the desirability of expelling the Poles. "Population exchanges" were carried out between Soviet Ukraine and Poland; "ethnic unmixing" was the spirit of the moment. Moscow sent Russians and Ukrainians from the east to help integrate Galicia and Volhynia; locals were to be made into Soviets. This social engineering project played out against the backdrop of a partisan war fought by the Ukrainian Insurgent Army against Soviet forces; the Ukrainian death toll from the Soviet counterinsurgency was approximately 112,000. In the end, the Soviets won.

After the war the Ukrainian Soviet Socialist Republic included the west Ukrainian lands of eastern Galicia and Volhynia, as well as Transcarpathian Ruthenia taken from Czechoslovakia, and northern Bukovina taken from Romania. It existed until 1991; that year the Soviet Union dissolved, and Ukraine—like Russia, Latvia, Lithuania, Estonia, and other former Soviet republics—became its own country. It was a revolutionary moment without a revolution. The Soviet Union was not overthrown; it collapsed. As a result of that collapse, Ukraine received independence. The most breathtaking social engineering experiment the world had known had come to an end.

Fantasies of Galicia

"Between myself and each new person the world begins anew, as if nothing up to this time had been established and decided," wrote Bruno Schulz.

Schulz, a Polish-Jewish artist and writer, was born in 1892 in an east Galician town named Drohobych. He is famous for his descriptions of the alluring "cinnamon shops" on the town's market square, blushing salesgirls, men in black bowler hats, bearded Jews in colored gabardines, prostitutes in lacey dresses who might be the wives of barbers, and his family's apartment "full of large closets, deep sofas, pale mirrors, and tacky artificial palms." In his stories seasons change, temperatures waver, and light trembles. The light is often dim and pale, the imagery often sensuous and tawdry: of crows, butterflies, and cockroaches; of milk cans, lamps, and combs; of thorny acacias and postage stamps of Emperor Franz Joseph. At times the details approach the repulsive in their lushness; at times Schulz lingers on the fragile border between the seductive and the grotesque.

In the story "August," Schulz describes walking with his mother in late summer on the market square "until finally on the corner of Stryjska Street we entered the shadow of the pharmacy. In the pharmacy's wide window a large bathtub full of raspberry juice symbolized the coolness of the balsams, which could soothe all sufferings." That story is set during Schulz's childhood, when Drohobych was still ruled by the Habsburgs, tucked in a region home to Polish-, Ukrainian-, Yiddish-, and German-speakers; to Roman Catholics, Greek Catholics, Armenian Catholics, Orthodox Christians, and Jews.

Habsburg Empress Maria Theresa had named "Galicia" the territory she impolitely took from the Polish-Lithuanian Commonwealth in the late eighteenth century. Galicia, Schulz's homeland, remained in the Empress's family until the Habsburg Empire ceased to exist. For a brief moment in late 1918 and early 1919, Drohobych found itself in the West Ukrainian People's Republic. During the years when Schulz was recalling the pharmacy on Stryjska Street, Drohobych belonged to independent Poland. In September 1939, the Red Army invaded eastern Poland, and Drohobych was annexed to Soviet Ukraine. In June 1941, Germany invaded the Soviet Union, and the Wehrmacht occupied Drohobych. Schulz was a Jew. For a time SS *Hauptscharführer* Felix Landau protected Schulz's life in exchange for Schulz painting scenes from fairy tales on the walls of his son's bedroom. Schulz painted until November 1942, when a Gestapo man shot him to death.

In February 2001, Jurko Prochasko, a Ukrainian translator and essayist, was among a small team assembled by the German filmmaker Benjamin Geissler that discovered the murals Bruno Schulz had painted for Landau. By then Drohobych belonged to independent Ukraine. Jurko had been skeptical when Geissler had called and asked for his help. "I'll find them," the filmmaker insisted. At the villa from whose balcony Landau once shot at passersby there lived an elderly woman, dressed in black, in mourning for her son. It was two days before what would have been his fiftieth birthday. The old woman did not know who Bruno Schulz was; even so, she allowed the visitors to come inside. The room Jurko entered was small. In the first moments the images on the wall were hazy, then with some labor they revealed themselves: a dancer and a gnome, a princess and a king, a coach and a rider. The head of a horse. A monster.

Bruno Schulz mattered to Jurko Prochasko: Schulz and his work belonged to a "lost paradise" named Galicia. It was the world Jurko had longed for as a child growing up in Ivano-Frankivsk, some eighty miles from Drohobych. By the time Jurko was born in 1970, Ivano-Frankivsk had been part of the Soviet Union for a quarter-century. Yet in his parents' apartment there remained "objects, everything that composed the texture of daily life . . . these were remnants of a lost paradise, which I summarized for myself with the mythical word 'Galicia.'" Although family history was important to his mother, and she told her sons about their grandparents and great-grandparents, Jurko's mother never suggested that this older world had been an idyllic one. Jurko conjured up that vision by himself. It seemed obvious to him that all things from that older world—buildings, objects, art, language—were superior to what had replaced them. At school he was taught that the Soviet Union had brought progress in every realm of life. Yet even as a child, Jurko could see that this was not progress but deterioration, above all an aesthetic and moral deterioration.

It was not only objects that summoned Jurko to this mythical Galicia. There were people, too, certain elderly people who spoke an archaic Ukrainian, whose eyes held a different expression, whose gesticulations and mannerisms all suggested that they were remnants of this lost world. The novelist Yuri Andrukhovych, older than Jurko by ten years, also grew up in Ivano-Frankivsk. He, too, noticed in his youth those elderly people who spoke a Galician dialect, remembered Latin proverbs from their school days, and dressed as if they were on their way to greet Habsburg Archduke Franz Ferdinand. Perhaps, Andrukhovych wrote, "they constituted some kind of secret association, an esoteric imperial-royal club named after Bruno Schulz." To him they appeared to be creatures from another planet. He was attentive to their existence, but he was not seduced by them. Jurko was; it was a libidinal attraction that was the counterpart of his visceral aversion to the "Sovietness that surrounded and washed away our archaic, museum-like Galicianness." He described his feelings towards the world these elderly people evoked: "'Idealization' would be too weak. I would rather say 'mystification,' or some kind of aspiration to transcendence . . . I would describe it in German as *Verlustlust*—that is, there's *Lust*, there's Eros, which cannot be gotten rid of, because it's everywhere, but that Eros is directed towards things that have already been lost."

Jurko himself did not imitate that prewar aesthetic. When we met in Lviv in April 2014, he was clean-shaven and wearing jeans; light brown hair fell into very bright blue eyes. His own work encompassed literature from the whole of the twentieth century: he translated Robert Musil, Joseph Roth, and Franz Kafka from German; Józef Wittlin, Jarosław Iwaszkiewicz, and Leszek Kołakowski from Polish; Debora Vogel from Yiddish. The Polish-Jewish poet Debora Vogel had been a close friend of Bruno Schulz. And like Schulz, Vogel was killed in 1942 by the Germans. Jurko's own essays were inflected with the timbres of all these voices. There was a kind of impassioned softness in his writing.

The historical milieu of which Jurko felt himself a part was embedded in that world of Bruno Schulz. It was a milieu whose existence was suspected by few: he was descended from the Uniate clerico-nobility, Greek Catholic Galician Ukrainians who had neither Polonized nor Russified, Ukrainophiles who embraced the liberal nationalism of the 1848 European revolutions. This tiny milieu—among the last handful of liberals in interwar Europe—never accepted the radical nationalism of Stepan Bandera and the Ukrainian Insurgent Army; never accepted their hostility towards Poles, Jews, and others; never accepted their use of terrorism and ethnic cleansing. That legacy was never their own.

"This all led to my growing up in a world of fantasized exclusivity," Jurko described. He felt that all that was best had been lost. He spent his youth persuaded that most people who belonged to the unaesthetic Soviet world could not understand him. Later, as an adult, Jurko went to Austria, where he was trained in psychoanalysis; he came to understand his feelings about belonging to a lost paradise as "a narcissistic fantasy" requiring reflection.

Jurko grew up speaking Ukrainian and Russian. He learned Polish and German because these were the Galician languages of his grandparents' time. His maternal grandparents had studied in Vienna; his grandmother had once practiced medicine in Vienna's nineteenth district. It was the money they earned there that allowed them to return to eastern Galicia and build the home where Jurko grew up. At that time, in the 1930s, everything about that building was modern: the Bauhaus architecture, the furniture, the central heating, the electricity, the lamps. His grandparents descended from the Ukrainian clerical nobility were bearers of European modernity.

In 1939 came the catastrophe. Together Nazism and Stalinism destroyed an entire world. And of that very small milieu—of that ethos of aristocratic, Greek Catholic, liberal Ukrainian patriotism—very little survived. His grandparents were the last generation with a taste for modernity—in contrast to Jurko himself.

"Because as a result of that loss, of that *Verlustlust*, I like only antiques."

Jurko's mother, born in 1940 during the Red Army's occupation of eastern Galicia, had always been a Ukrainian patriot. As a girl growing up during late Stalinism she saw the disaster that Soviet rule was for her family: their property was expropriated; some relatives were shot; others lost their minds in prison. Even so, she wanted very much to sing the beautiful songs and believe that the Soviet Union wished for peace throughout the world. To Jurko she was deeply good, and deeply naïve. He described her as "an orchid, an orchid of catastrophe."

Jurko's father was different. He came not from the Greek Catholic nobility, but from an upwardly mobile, Ukrainophile family whose property was confiscated by the Bolsheviks. Jurko's great-grandfather was an engineer who, together with his daughter and grandson—Jurko's father—was sent to the gulag in 1948. Jurko's father was then eight years old; he grew up in Stalin's camps, where adolescents were already criminals. In the gulag, teenage boys would play cards, and the winners would select a stranger whom the loser would have to kill. The one who lost would have to enter a room where a film was being shown and stab to death, for instance, the person who was sitting in the first seat in the fourth row.

And so in contrast to Jurko's mother, Jurko's father never had any illusions about the Soviet world. Yet he was the one who joined the Communist Party. It was a gesture of pragmatic conformity. He and Jurko's mother lived in an apartment in the Bauhaus-style stone building her parents had built in the 1930s. He provided for them. He had grown up in the gulag; he understood well what happened to people who opposed the Soviet regime, and he did not want that, not for himself and not for his family. And Jurko loved his father, although in his eyes his father was a traitor. It was his mother's world—the world that had brought fin-de-siècle Viennese modernism to eastern Galicia—he idealized.

"I didn't understand then, that in my father there was much vitality, and on the other side there was much morbidity. But I preferred the noble morbidity to the opportunistic vitality."

Jurko himself never believed in the Soviet promise. The libidinal identification with the bygone Galician world was too absorbing, the Soviet world too repelling. When at seventeen Jurko left home, it was to study German philology in Lviv. At that time, 1987, the possibility of meeting an actual German was remote; German literature was a purely idealistic undertaking— an attempt to connect with that no-longer-existing world in which German had been the language of high culture. Once

Lviv had been the capital of Austrian Galicia; to Jurko it was the "epicenter of the cosmos." To reach Lviv was like reaching Jerusalem. By then the reformer Mikhail Gorbachev had come to power in the Soviet Union; it was the time of *glasnost* and *perestroika.*

"And it was all at the right moment," he described, "because just at this time comes sexuality, the desire for emancipation from the father, first love, dreams about the future, Gorbachev."

It meant the possibility of change, and of liberation. There were thousands of demonstrations—protests against atomic energy in the wake of the 1986 nuclear disaster at Chernobyl, marches and rallies in support of the Ukrainian language, the Greek Catholic Church, Ukrainian independence. Jurko took part in all of it; those demonstrations were his civic education.

At the time, at the end of the 1980s, Jurko had believed that what was happening in Ukraine was just like what was happening in Poland, Czechoslovakia, Hungary, and elsewhere in Eastern Europe. He did not foresee the persistence of Sovietness. He did not see that Ukraine was different, that the Soviet Union was different even from its communist satellites. Perhaps, he now thought, if everyone had been bearers of that bygone Galician world, Ukraine would have had a revolution like the one Poland had in 1989. But there were too few emissaries of that world.

Instead, in December 1991, Leonid Kravchuk, a member of the Communist Party for over three decades, became the first president of independent Ukraine. "How was it possible to vote for Kravchuk, who was a continuation, who was the secretary of ideology in the Communist Party, who was in the Politburo of Soviet Ukraine?" Jurko asked himself in 1991, "and that *he* became president of independent Ukraine—for me this was a profanity." That was the moment when he realized that no, this was not Czechoslovakia where Václav Havel was elected, or Poland where Lech Wałęsa was elected; this was someplace else—and "we will suffer for a long, long, long time in this post-Soviet purgatory."

Jurko had hoped that Ukraine would join Europe. Yet there were, as it turned out, more voices on behalf of Soviet continuity. Jurko's was not an easy position: to reject continuity with communism; to reject Moscow as "hostile, brutal and merciless"; to reject the cult of Stepan Bandera and the Ukrainian Insurgent Army. It was not easy to live ensconced in nostalgia for a world that had ceased to exist long before his own birth; to cling to a liberal nationalism whose moment had passed before it was ever realized; to insist on a gentle, anti-imperial patriotism, a vision of the Ukrainian nation realizing itself harmoniously within a cosmopolitan Ukrainian state. And it was not easy to find oneself on "Europe's forgotten fringes," kept at a distance by those securely in Europe's center. Not being wanted was not a very nice feeling, wrote Jurko in 2011.

The Revolutions That Were Not

Jurko's first revolutionary moment—the breakup of the Soviet Union—had been a coming of age story. To be twenty-one years old in 1991 had felt serendipitous. What followed felt much less so. In the 1990s Leonid Kuchma came to power and led what the political scientist Keith Darden named a "blackmail state." In 2004, Kuchma's chosen successor, Viktor Yanukovych, declared victory in the presidential elections over his opponent, Viktor Yushchenko. Yanukovych, a criminal with robbery convictions, represented post-Soviet corruption, oligarchy, gangsterism. Yushchenko, who had been head of the Central Bank, appeared to stand for democracy, the rule of law, a step towards Europe. Yanukovych's alleged victory involved the poisoning of Yushchenko with dioxin—and election fraud.

In November 2004 thousands of Ukrainians went to the Maidan Nezalezhnosti, Independence Square, to protest rigged elections. Located at the end of Khreshchatyk, Kiev's largest shopping boulevard, the Maidan had not long before undergone an aesthetic transformation. The twentieth century had ended; the grayness of communism, of socialist realism, of Sovietness was cast off. Now glass domes emerged from under the ground onto the square, protruding ceilings of a subterranean shopping center. It was a time for bourgeois boutiques—and for brighter colors. In the first year of the new millennium, builders completed a replica of a medieval Kievan city gate in dandelion yellow. Atop the gate, the archangel Michael stood poised with sword, shield, and halo, his gold-plated wings spread wide. That same year, 2001, a victory monument was unveiled in celebration of the tenth anniversary of Ukraine's independence: a two-hundred-foot-tall column faced with white Italian marble. Atop the column, the artist who had created the archangel Michael had sculpted the Slavic goddess Berehynia, bearing a guelder rose branch. Michael and Berehynia were a natural couple: robust and statuesque, cast in bronze.

Unlike Lviv, Kiev was not quaint, and its Maidan was not charming like the central squares in smaller cities. Imposing Soviet-era buildings surrounded a multileveled urban space. The glass domes behind the medieval gate suggested awkwardness, but also capacious eclecticism. This capaciousness reflected, too, sheer size: the Maidan was a spacious agora, tents needed not feel cramped there. For three weeks in late autumn 2004, Ukrainians stayed on the Maidan and froze.

The "Orange Revolution" was bloodless. It was also victorious: another round of elections was held in late December 2004; and in January 2005 Yushchenko was inaugurated as Ukrainian president. "Yulia, the Gas Princess," the glamorous oligarch Yulia Tymoshenko, who wore her blonde hair in a peasant-style braid wrapped around her head, had long played a vocal role in the opposition to Kuchma. Now she became Yushchenko's prime minister. Happy and satisfied, everyone went home.

In Lviv one of those most active in the Orange Revolution was the physicist Ivan Vakarchuk. His eldest son, Slava, was a rock star, the lead singer of the wildly popular band Okean Elzy. In Slava's description, his father had been neither a communist believer nor a dissident, "just a wise, sound, I think highly moral guy," who during Soviet times quietly attended church. In the late 1980s, Ivan Vakarchuk had begun to talk to his then-teenage son about politics. Ivan could no longer wait: this was the moment when previously banned literature "came like an avalanche": Vladimir Nabokov, Aleksandr Solzhenitsyn, Mikhail Bulgakov's *Master and Margarita*. "Out of the blue," it seemed to Slava, his physics professor father became a politician: in 1989 Ivan Vakarchuk was elected a deputy to the Supreme Soviet in Moscow.

Two years later, during a visit to the United States, Ivan Vakarchuk was introduced as a Soviet politician.

No—he corrected his hosts—there no longer was any such country.

In December 1991 the Soviet Union formally ceased to exist. Ivan Vakarchuk returned from Moscow and assumed the rectorship of Lviv University. He was still rector in 2004, when he threw his energy into a revolution that appeared to be a great success.

Yet the Orange Revolution's victory proved false. Viktor Yushchenko and Yulia Tymoshenko soon became enemies. Europe was not welcoming; Ukraine was not forthcoming with reforms. The reign of oligarchy and corruption continued. In an attempt to move away from Moscow, Yushchenko turned towards memory politics: not only honoring the victims of the *Holodomor*, the famine of the 1930s, but also celebrating the Organization of Ukrainian Nationalists as a symbol of struggle against Russian imperialism. In January 2010, he conferred "Hero of Ukraine," the highest state honor, posthumously upon the fascist Stepan Bandera.

Slava did not recall ever having been awed by Yushchenko. He thought of himself as "rather cynical," even though he was a lyrical songwriter. Or rather, although his heart was lyrical, his brain was cynical.

"My mom is a very artistic person, my dad is a very analytical person, so I'm half and half," Slava explained. "Many people say it's a very strange and very rare mixture."

It was true: Slava was very sensitive; he was moved by beautiful music, by human pain, by partings with friends. He was a man who was unashamed to cry. Yet he was also very sober about the human condition and its vulnerability to weakness, selfishness, irresponsibility. Slava went to the streets during the Orange Revolution above all to protest election fraud. He was hopeful about Yushchenko, but soon realized that for real change Ukrainians would have to wait a little longer.

"But that was not his personal blame," Slava said of Yushchenko. "The civil society was not ready for different leaders. They were still longing for the messiah. So they wanted Yushchenko to become a good tsar, and he wanted himself to become a good tsar."

Jurko Prochasko was self-critical about these yearnings for a good tsar. The Orange Revolution had been a naïve revolution, he came to understand, psychologically immature.

"We were convinced then," Jurko said, "that we can delegate to one person and he's good, so it's ideal, he'll do everything. We concluded the revolution in three weeks, delegated everything to him, and went away. In that sense Yushchenko's betrayal was a very, very valuable experience. . . . At the time we thought there was a bad father, and we had to replace the bad father with a good father. And now we no longer believe in a father at all."

Not all was lost. Not only was the disillusionment with Yushchenko a "cure for paternalism," but the experience of masses of people taking to the streets so quickly was also a source of empowerment. To his friends who had become skeptical Jurko began to say, "You'll be surprised. One right moment and everyone will be mobilized." After all, it had already happened twice in his lifetime. If it had happened twice, it could happen again.

"Likes" Don't Count

Viktor Yushchenko and Yulia Tymoshenko were such disappointments that in the 2010 elections Yanukovych returned to defeat Tymoshenko—whom he then put in prison. Yanukovych's base of support came from eastern and southern Ukraine; he himself was a son of the east Ukrainian mining region called the Donbas. To many there, Yanukovych was a local boy who had made it in the world. Of course "no one really loves him," of course he was slimy, ridiculous, and uneducated, a working-class hoodlum-turned-kleptocratic parvenu with appalling taste in art, but still—Jurko speculated—the thinking in the Donbas was that he was *svoi*, one of us. And maybe that was a source of pride. To some he seemed to offer stability, even if of a curious sort, given that under his rule conditions for workers in the Donbas remained abysmal. Yanukovych and his mafia-like "Family" of political allies built golden villas while ordinary people starved and froze and died in explosions at unregulated mines. Gangsters blackmailed small businesses, extracting money in exchange for tolerating their existence. In many small towns and villages it was understood that order was maintained by a local *smotriashchii*—literally, "one who is looking," a representative of a mafia group who controlled a given area and extorted money. Yanukovych himself offered no grand narrative, no promise of transcendence, no story about a higher purpose of present suffering. He was nakedly, unapologetically a gangster.

("It's not just that he's a gangster," my friend Ivan Krastev, a political analyst, said to me. "It's that he's a *petty* gangster." To that thought Polish foreign minister Radosław Sikorski responded, "Well, the sums involved were not petty.")

Ukraine had never had the rule of law. Yet under Yanukovych the kleptocracy was particularly shameless; the judicial system made itself available for private hire; the police functioned according to the principle of arbitrariness. Slava Vakarchuk believed that Ukrainians had gotten what they had chosen for themselves.

"I think that Yanukovych won elections fairly," Slava told me, "and we paid a very high price for that. But that was a fair price for Ukrainian society. Because they elected him and they needed to live through this mistake."

Yet the hundreds of thousands who had taken part in the Orange Revolution did not go back out on the streets. It might have seemed that the time for revolution was over, that people had resigned themselves to this post-Soviet purgatory—until the moment in November 2013 when Yanukovych unexpectedly refused to sign an association agreement with the European Union. Russian president Vladimir Putin was pressuring Yanukovych to join his Eurasian Union, to ally with the *russkii mir*, "the Russian world," against the West. Even so, Yanukovych's refusal to sign the association agreement was very abrupt: even while his 2010 victory had clearly represented rapprochement with Russia, the Ukrainian president's rhetoric had consistently promoted some form of European integration, in particular an agreement to lessen trade barriers and enable visa-free travel for Ukrainians in the Schengen zone. The long-awaited signing ceremony in Vilnius had already been arranged when Yanukovych suddenly changed his mind. The association agreement was far from ideal: it promised no eventual acceptance into the European Union, obliged Ukraine to undertake costly reforms, and was likely to provoke financial retaliation from Russia. Nonetheless it was of tremendous symbolic importance: would Ukraine have a chance to belong to Europe—or not?

In Jurko's mind, of course the agreement was not fantastic. Of course it was largely symbolic. But it was *something*, a sign that Ukraine would, even if slowly, embark on a different path, that even though Yanukovych might remain a repulsive despot, he would have to submit, for instance, to a reform of the justice system. It would have meant that even this oligarchical regime was conceding to depart from its most ostentatious kleptocratic practices. It would have been "a foot in the door" of Europe.

When on 21 November 2013 Yanukovych refused to sign the association agreement, Jurko's friends oscillated between a feeling that the end of the world had come and a feeling that no, they would not take this, they had reached their limit. Around eight o'clock that evening a thirty-two-year-old Afghan-Ukrainian journalist named Mustafa Nayyem, who had reported on xenophobia and corruption for the news site *Ukrayinska Pravda*, posted a note on his Facebook page: "Come on, let's get serious. Who is ready to go out to the Maidan by midnight tonight? 'Likes' don't count."

Jurko's eleven-year-old son drew a European flag and wrote on it "*Ukraina—Unia.*" Jurko took him to the central square in Lviv, the small Maidan, where people gathered around the monument to the nineteenth century Ukrainian poet Taras Shevchenko. In the beginning they were mostly young people: "Euromaidan" belonged to the students. Perhaps in the short term they had the most at stake: access to Schengen zone visas, scholarships, internships, opportunities to study abroad. Would Europe be open to them, or not?

They were the iPhone generation who—unlike Jurko's generation, who had seen the Soviet Union fall in their twenties, who had ushered Yushchenko into the presidency in their thirties —had not yet had their chance at revolution. They were tired

of politicians and political parties. ("It's interesting," said Katia
Mishchenko, a young Ukrainian translator of Walter Benjamin
and Theodor Adorno, "because no one is waiting for Yulia.")
They were "indifferent to political parties, but not to politics,"
explained Taras Dobko, a philosopher in his early forties who
was vice-rector of the Ukrainian Catholic University in Lviv.
Many of them were his own students. One of them was Markiyan Prochasko, Jurko's nephew.

Markiyan, like his uncle, had soft, unkempt hair that fell into
his eyes. There was something delicate about him—he was thin
and kind and looked even younger than his age. On 21 November Markiyan read Mustafa Nayyem's Facebook appeal, and late
at night got on his bicycle and rode from the outskirts of Lviv
to the Shevchenko monument in the city center. He and other
students stood in the circle, held hands, and shouted "Ukraine
is Europe!" Some of the students had come with the young university lecturer Bohdan Solchanyk, who told them that night:
you're shouting "revolution," but you can't make a revolution in
one day. The next day they came back.

Markiyan spent the following three nights on this small
Maidan in Lviv. On the fourth day he decided to go to Kiev, several hours away by train. Student groups were organizing trips,
but Markiyan wanted to go alone. When he arrived in Kiev the
Maidan seemed sad to him, terrible in a way, not very many
people were there, and he despaired that nobody cared about

the situation in Ukraine. A few hours passed. In the evening he saw that more and more people were coming, and then he felt happiness—that they were there, that he was there.

Jurko did not feel the same happiness that his nephew did. "I experienced no excitement," he told me.

None. When I went to the revolution on the Maidan, whether I went to Kiev or here in Lviv, there was no euphoria and no desire. I didn't shout anything . . . I was simply silent. I always understood it as hard, unpleasant, draining, but necessary work. Simply work. I didn't like freezing, I didn't like standing, I don't very much like crowds. . . . I knew that I had to do it, although from time to time I would ask myself: what am I, an old guy, doing here? Why am I taking their revolution from them? It's important that they have their own revolution.

Jurko's colleague, thirty-nine-year-old Serhiy Zhadan, was a very different kind of writer. "When I was fourteen and had my own views about life, I first loaded up on alcohol," begins his novel *Depeche Mode*, "Up to the gills. It was really hot and the blue heavens swam above me, and I lay dying on a striped mattress and couldn't even get drunk, because I was only four-teen and simply didn't know how." His novels are filled with lost young people, with vodka, sex, and rock and roll—none of which is sexy. (This is in contrast to the novelist himself. One Polish journalist who attended Serhiy Zhadan's poetry read-ing in Warsaw commented that he had never seen so many young women wearing short skirts in March.) There was something in his novels akin to the Beat Poets, characters from towns in post-Soviet eastern Ukraine reminiscent of Jack Kerouac and Neal Cassady. Notwithstanding their very different literary sensibilities, Serhiy had the same feeling as Jurko did when the students began demonstrating in November.

"It's good," Serhiy told a friend in Poland, "that they've taken the matter in hand, that they've organized themselves. For them we belong among the old irons, we're worn out, we've exhausted our use. This is their chance and their revolution."

The political scientist Mykola Riabchuk's son, Yuri, a punk rock drummer in his mid-twenties, looked exactly like his father, uncannily so. Yuri had gone to the Maidan in Kiev that first week just to see what was happening there. Some activists got in touch with him: could he loan his amplifiers to the Euromaidan? Yuri talked to his father: he was young and did not have much money, the amplifiers were expensive. Mykola offered paternal support—and insurance: if the amplifiers got destroyed, he would replace them.

Some activists got in touch with Slava Vakarchuk as well, although not to ask for amplifiers. They wanted him to give a speech: Slava was a rock star, people would listen to him. He agreed to the speech, although he did not want to talk about the European Union. For Slava, being part of Europe had little to do with Yanukovych's signing or not signing an association agreement. Being a part of Europe, he told the young people, was a question of values: the value of freedom of choice, the value of dignity.

"Don't give up, everything is only beginning." These were Slava's last words to them on 28 November.

"Unfortunately," Slava told me much later, "not only good things began after that."

Fathers and Sons

After Slava Vakarchuk's speech on 28 November 2013, Misha Martynenko stayed on the Maidan until the next morning. He remembered the Maidan as it was that evening as a youthful place, cheerful, with music and dancing.

"It felt really peaceful," Yustyna Kravchuk, a film studies student, described those days and nights in November.

Markiyan Prochasko also spent the night after Slava's speech on the Maidan. The following night he was so tired that he went to a friend's apartment to sleep. When Markiyan left the Maidan around 2 am, several hundred people were still there. Two hours later riot police, called *Berkut*, arrived with tear gas and truncheons. The *Berkutovtsy* beat the students, the women as well, and the others there with them, including the Armenian painter Boris Yeghiazaryan and an elderly former officer in the Soviet army.

Markiyan's father, the novelist Taras Prochasko, knew his son was in Kiev, and he was proud of Markiyan. Taras was thinking about the early 1990s, when he had been at the demonstrations from the very first days, when his own parents had not held him back: they had understood that he needed to take part in the end of the Soviet Union. And now he understood that Markiyan needed to have this experience.

"Every generation should live through its own revolution," Taras told me. It did not seem right to interfere.

Taras Prochasko was at home in Ivano-Frankivsk on 30 November when his phone rang at 6 am. A girl whom he barely knew was calling; she had called Taras because he was the only person older than student-age whose number was saved on her phone. She was distraught, talking quickly about a pogrom, victims, asking him to tell people what had happened. Then came the paternal anxiety: why had this girl, and not Markiyan, called him? What had happened to his son? Markiyan was not answering his phone. Taras started to make phone calls to Kiev, to hospitals and police stations, to friends who were doctors. For hours he searched and waited. He was prepared for the worst.

It was close to noon when Markiyan woke up. He switched on his phone and saw that some of his friends had called over forty times. He began returning the calls—to his father, his mother, his girlfriend, who posted on Facebook that Markiyan was okay. That same day Taras left Ivano-Frankivsk to join Markiyan in Kiev. He drove all through the night, and when he arrived in the morning there were already hundreds of thousands of people on the streets. Taras understood then that whatever was to happen, whether or not the protests would succeed, something had now changed in his country.

On 30 November the novelist Yuri Andrukhovych was at the Lviv airport waiting for his flight to Vienna when he learned that the students in Kiev had been beaten. He did not get on the plane. Instead he left the airport and went on to Kiev. Yanukovych had broken an unspoken social contract: in the two decades since independence, the government had never used this kind of violence against its own citizens.

People could not believe, Markiyan wrote to me, that something so brutal had happened not in Belarus or Kazakhstan or Russia, but in Ukraine. Some students were hospitalized. Others fled to the monastery on Saint Michael's Square, half a mile away. That Saturday, 30 November, more and more people gathered in front of the baby blue cathedral with the golden dome. Markiyan was among them. All through the following night people came and brought warm food; they stood on the square to protect the students hiding in the monastery.

Jurko's friend Ola Hnatiuk, a literary critic and Polish translator of Ukrainian literature, called a friend at dawn the next day. Ola's friend had already been standing for hours on Saint Michael's Square; she was freezing and could not move her fingers. Ola came to help; she sliced sandwiches while another friend, an editor, made coffee and tea. A woman standing next to them was distributing six liters of hot soup. After an hour or so, the woman who had brought the soup told Ola she had to leave: she had left a small child alone in their apartment. It was only then that Ola saw that the woman was also in an advanced stage of pregnancy.

The spontaneous self-organization impressed even those on the other side. Markiyan overheard a conversation between two of Yanukovych's supporters, well-dressed men, at Kiev's central train station: "People are bringing blankets, clothing—in bulk— to Saint Michael's Square . . . they have enormous cauldrons of potatoes and porridge. A huge amount of lard. There's tea, coffee, *sugar! Pickles! Jars full of honey!!! Condensed milk! And so many sausages!!!*"

For Jurko the brutality against the students was the end of his own ambivalence. Until that weekend Jurko had kept a certain distance: his generation had already had two chances. It was no longer his turn. On 30 November everything changed. Suddenly it was clear: it was everybody's turn.

Misha Martynenko had never seen as many people in one place as he saw on 1 December.

This was the day Euromaidan became "Maidan," with no prefix. Slava Vakarchuk, who had been ambivalent about Ukraine's readiness to join the European Union, now came every day. He understood that this was no longer merely about an association agreement with the European Union. "Maidan" had become an impassioned protest against brutality, corruption, and rule by gangsters. It had become a revolt against *proizvol*—a Russian word combining arbitrariness and tyranny, the condition of being made an object of someone else's will.

("It's a feeling of defenselessness," Victoria Narizhna, an activist from Dnipropetrovsk, explained, "in the face of . . ."

"The state," her husband, Ihor Petrovsky, finished her sentence.)

"In fact we live in a country where the level of civic life has been halted at the stage of banditry," Taras Prochasko had written a few years earlier. Now the slogan became "Away with the bandits!"

Jurko understood Yanukovych as a psychopath, pathologically lacking in empathy. For Yanukovych the Maidan was nothing more than a power game: *Kto kogo?* in Lenin's formulation. *Who imposes his will on whom?* On 30 November Yanukovych was counting on parents to drag their children off the streets. He miscalculated.

Many parents were thinking about the Gorbachev era. In 1988, two years after the nuclear disaster at Chernobyl, then fourteen-year-old Taras Ratushnyy had taken part in his first street action, an ecological protest. Schoolchildren practiced military exercises then, and Taras Ratushnyy and three of his friends smuggled their gas masks out of school. At the rally they put on their masks and carried banners with the slogan "Let's bury the remains of Chernobyl in the Kremlin wall!" His parents were there; his father turned white.

A quarter-century had passed since then. Now parents like Taras Ratushnyy and Taras Prochasko did not drag their sons and daughters off the streets. Instead they joined them there. Veterans of the Soviet war in Afghanistan—the *Afgantsy*, middle-aged men with combat experience—came to the Maidan to defend the students.

"There was a feeling that we are taxpayers, we pay to have the police protect us," the philosopher Taras Dobko explained, "and now we see what the main task of the police is: to beat our kids."

"We will protect our children," became the slogan—even of those who did not have children themselves. "It cannot be permitted," Markiyan remembered two elderly women, one speaking Ukrainian and one speaking Russian, saying in Kiev. *We cannot let them beat our children.*

One of those beaten children was Taras Ratushnyy's sixteen-year-old son. Roman Ratushnyy's shoulder had been battered, but he was not scared away, he stayed on the Maidan.

"Your mother must have been very upset," I said. "But she let you go back?"

"My mother was making Molotov cocktails on Hrushevskyi Street."

Self-Organization

This was when the difficult, draining months began. *"The troops guard their king, and we're going/to the revolution as if to our jobs,"* wrote the young poet Vasyl Lozynskyi. Jurko, too, went to the revolution as if reporting for service. He would have preferred to be doing something else—but it was impossible to do anything else.

The beaten students had become "our children," Iryna Iaremko, a middle-aged real estate agent, explained to me in Lviv. After 30 November, from her improvised headquarters at the Viennese Café behind the Taras Shevchenko monument, Iryna spent every day organizing buses to take people from Lviv to the Maidan in Kiev. She and her fellow volunteers did not advertise their services. People came looking for them, thousands and thousands of people, not only from Lviv, but also from the surrounding Galician villages, all looking for a way to get to Kiev.

For those who boarded the buses, going to the Maidan meant not only taking part in a demonstration, but also entering an alternate world, "passionate and motley in its social and ideological composition," in the description of Nelia Vakhovska, a young editor and translator. Markiyan described how the borders that normally existed between people dissolved; it became very easy to talk to strangers. The Maidan was a "laboratory of the social contract," in one writer's description, "a union of IT specialists from Dnipropetrovsk and a Hutsul shepherd, an Odessa mathematician and a Kiev businessman, a translator from Lviv and a Tatar peasant from Crimea." On the Maidan—Victoria Narizhna and Ihor Petrovsky suspected—many urban men and women with doctorates were having conversations with peasants for the first time in their lives, and vice versa.

The Maidan was a rarely encountered feat of civil society: not only a protest movement, but also a parallel *polis*. By the time Victoria and Ihor arrived from Dnipropetrovsk to the Maidan in Kiev on 4 December, the kitchens were already working; the infrastructure was in place. Musicians performed, artists painted, physicians treated the injured. Ruslana, the pop star with the irresistibly warm smile who won the 2004 Eurovision Song Contest, was there from the very beginning, leading the crowd in jumping up and down to stay warm. There was a library, an Open University with lectures and film screenings, and a communal upright piano painted yellow and blue. People erected tents, built bonfires, and cooked soup in iron cauldrons. Donations were abundant. Food, clothing, and medicine were distributed without charge. Volunteers cleared snow and ice. For Katia Mishchenko, a young leftist, this was the communist dream fulfilled: "From each according to his ability, to each according to his need." Organized volunteer units of *Samooborona*, "self-defense," served as ersatz police protection. ("It was a pleasure, understanding you have real protectors on the streets," the student Mariya Borysova told me.) An LGBT organization transformed its confidential hotline into an emergency hotline for the Maidan.

"People are never as well organized as they are during a revolution," wrote Sławomir Sierakowski, a left-wing public intellectual in Poland. "Anyone who saw the kitchens at Euromaidan knows what this means."

To Victoria and Ihor it felt as if they were entering another world, a world that was well kept and unsoiled, a world where responsibility had developed organically.

"You go behind the barricades and you find yourself in a completely different space," described Victoria, "because where you just were there was garbage and dirt, whereas here Ukrainians feel that they're at home, and not a single scrap of paper falls to the ground."

"The Maidan was so clean you could eat off the asphalt," Misha Martynenko told me.

Nothing like this had ever happened before.

The Bell Tower

On the night of 10 December Yanukovych tried again to clear the Maidan. Thousands of *Berkutovtsy*, riot policemen, with armored vehicles approached; they began to break down the barricades. At Saint Michael's Cathedral, at one in the morning, twenty-five-year-old Father Ivan Sydor made a decision to sound an alarm: for four hours the bells tolled in the spire, the sound resonating throughout central Kiev. It was the first time the monastery had used its bell tower for this purpose since the Mongols invaded Kiev in the 1240s.

Watching on television at a friend's Kiev apartment, Markiyan thought this was the end of the revolution. Then he went outside and saw people from all over the city heading to the Maidan. Markiyan joined them. The atmosphere was changing very quickly, it could shift in a moment—from calm to anxious, from peaceful to violent.

"I am not very strong," Markiyan said to me.

He was in the middle of the Maidan, where women and the elderly and others who were not very strong were protected by those on the periphery. In any case, he was with the writers Yuri Andrukhovych and Oleksandr Boichenko, friends of his father, who would not have let him go where it was more dangerous.

After midnight the philologist Ola Hnatiuk received a text message from a friend on the Maidan. Berkut was preparing to attack, Ola's friend wrote. On Ola's street, twenty or so yards from the building where she lived, Ola saw three parked buses with *titushki*—thugs hired by Yanukovych. She grasped the situation at once: the plan was to chase the protestors from the Maidan, then beat them as they tried to escape. In the early hours of the morning Ola managed to reach the Maidan together with two friends: a literary publisher named Leonid Finberg and his wife, Lena, a physician, both in their sixties. In the middle of the night Lena had turned on her computer and seen the Facebook post from her son, Arseniy: he was leaving by car for the Maidan and offered to take along others. Lena posted that she and her husband were going, too. They picked up Ola, a petite woman of fifty-two, who next to Leonid and Lena looked young and strong. Ola was a Polish citizen; her older friends were both Jews; all three were Ukrainian patriots. Lena, "the gentlest creature in the world," as Ola described her, was a slightly plump woman less than five feet tall who walked with a limp. Ola had to pull her away from the riot policemen, because Lena felt compelled to tell each one of them how she felt about what he was doing.

Like Markiyan and Ola and Lena and Leonid, Slava Vakarchuk also spent the night of 10–11 December on the Maidan. There he saw his band's former guitarist; the breakup had not been very amicable, Slava and the guitarist had not remained friends. Yet finding each other that night, they embraced and decided to play a concert there a few days later with Okean Elzy's old lineup.

"Were you ever afraid when you were on the Maidan?" I asked Slava.

"No," he told me, "you're never afraid when you're there. You're afraid before you go there. When you're there you're not afraid anymore."

I asked Markiyan, too, if he had been afraid. He had been much more nervous watching on television, he answered. This was something he and his friends all agreed upon: when they watched the news on television, they were much more frightened than when they were actually there, actually in danger. Taras Ratushnyy and his son Roman had the same experience: watching television made them too nervous. They felt safe only on the Maidan.

On this night of 10 December Yanukovych's second attempt

to clear the Maidan failed. By Christmas time people of all generations were coming there. Yuri Andrukhovych came with his wife and daughter. Mariya Borysova, a student in Kiev, went with her father. He had been drawn there himself from the beginning; he wanted, too, to protect his daughter, who suspected this had something to do with masculinity. She and her father would walk to the Maidan together, and once there, go their separate ways: she with her friends, he with his. It was on the walk there that she needed her father's protection, Mariya explained; on the Maidan itself she felt secure. Her friends often came with their parents; sometimes the families all went together. One day, when it was calm on the Maidan, Mariya's father brought with them her seven-year-old brother and her elderly grandmother. From that moment on, Mariya wrote to me, her grandmother understood completely what the Maidan was and why her family was there—which was, her granddaughter added, not easy for a teacher of Russian literature from the Soviet Union.

Four days after Berkut's failed attack, on 14 December, some 250,000 people gathered on the Maidan for Okean Elzy's concert. Some had come from the "anti-Maidan," the pro-government rallies organized in nearby Mariinskyi Park and European Square; the band had even saved places for their fans on the other side, because Slava did not want anyone to feel excluded. Okean Elzy's 2005 song "*Ia ne zdamsia bez boiu*"—"I won't give up without a fight"—recounted scenes of pouring glasses of wine with honey; the lyrics suggested a man struggling with a destructive love affair. On the Maidan the meaning changed: "Without a Fight" became a theme song of the revolution. It was not the only one. Okean Elzy's 2001 wake-up song, "*Vstavai!*"—"Get up!"—now sounded prophetic:

> *Vstavai! Myla moia, vstavai!*
> *Myla moia, vstavai! Myla moia, vstavai!*
> *Davai! Myla moia, davai! Myla moia, davai!*
> *Bil'shoho vymahai!*
>
> *Get up! My darling, get up!*
> *Get up, my darling! My darling, get up!*
> *Let's go! Let's go, my darling! My darling, let's go!*
> *Demand more! And show—*

Okean Elzy's music reached back to an earlier pop-rock, melodic and guitar-driven. Slava's voice was gravelly and intense. In that earnest voice there was something buoyant and mobilizing, but also steadying and euphonic. It was freezing in Kiev; the steam from Slava's breath filled the stage like a fog machine. Slava was thin, strong, aerobic. He bounced like Tigger, as if the stage were a trampoline. By the concert's end it was nineteen degrees Fahrenheit, and Slava was wearing a t-shirt.

"It was great," Slava told me later, "it was cold, but I didn't feel cold."

Noah's Ark

People came to the Maidan to see what was there and ended up staying. One of them was Natan Khazin, a young rabbi from Odessa who had emigrated to Israel years earlier. Khazin, a broad-shouldered man with a crew cut and a trimmed beard, served in the Israeli Defense Forces, in the Gaza Strip, before friends in Ukraine convinced him to leave the war zone that was the Middle East and come to peaceful Kiev. ("Jewish luck," my Russian colleague commented.)

After the students were beaten on 30 November, Natan Khazin came to the Maidan as an observer. He wandered upon some men who were planning on storming a building. What was the constellation of forces? he asked them. How many men were defending the building? How many would carry out the attack? Did they know that in order to storm a building when both sides were equally armed they needed three times as many men on the offensive side? No, they did not have any idea. They could see, though, that Khazin did. Soon he was commanding several operations—and he came to realize that this was his war. He broke the Sabbath for the first time in his adult life. He felt no ambivalence about this: he was protecting civilian lives. He and other Ukrainian Jews taking part in the revolution began describing themselves as "*Zhidobandera.*"

The untranslatable "*Zhidobandera*" meant something like "Yid-Banderite;" and appreciating the phrase required a refined sense of irony. It also required a dialectical imagination that allowed the pejorative to be transformed into the affirmative: "*Zhid,*" in both Russian and Ukrainian, was a derogatory word for "Jew." Yanukovych and Putin had declared the protestors to be fascists, antisemites, and *Banderovtsy*, followers of the late Stepan Bandera. Jurko was dumbfounded: he, who felt nothing in common with Bandera's legacy at all. One slogan of the Maidan was "*Slava Ukraini—heroyam slava!*" *Glory to Ukraine— glory to the heroes!* This had once, seventy-some years earlier, been the slogan of the Ukrainian Insurgent Army, a paramilitary group associated with Stepan Bandera's faction of the Organization of Ukrainian Nationalists. After Germany invaded the Soviet Union in June 1941 and the Wehrmacht arrived in western Ukraine, more than a few followers of Stepan Bandera had taken the initiative in killing Jews.

Ola Hnatiuk, herself a Pole, was persuaded that no one any

longer understood the slogan in its radical nationalist context, that only the anti-imperial, anti-Soviet ethos of the words had remained.

"A lot of people in my generation don't know who Bandera is," Markiyan told me, "and that's okay, I think."

The Ukrainian historian Yaroslav Hrytsak described the Maidan as akin to Noah's Ark: it took "two of every kind." This was a revolution that was "maximally open," Jurko explained, and tolerated very different programs—there were liberals and socialists and nationalists and lunatics. At the same time, he pointed out, the "existential tolerance for such polyglossia, ideological polyphony" did not tell the whole story. There were real differences and real tensions, for instance between the leftists and the nationalist far Right like Svoboda ("Freedom") and Pravyi Sektor ("Right Sector").

I asked Jurko if he had had any contact with them.

"No, no," he answered. "How would I?"

After all—he explained—in this way revolution was just like ordinary life: people went to the revolution with their own friends.

"When Western audiences saw reports about militarized protesters wrapped in EU flags professing nationalist views," wrote the young leftist filmmaker Oleksiy Radynski,

> they experienced a kind of a cognitive dissonance. The immediate Western response was hypocritically colonial, proclaiming that Ukrainian protesters were not European enough to claim

allegiance to European values. In reality, the juxtaposition of neo-Nazi symbols with EU flags in the streets of Kyiv exemplified a pan-European malady. . . . If members of the racist and xenophobic extreme Right sit in nearly every one of the European parliaments, why are we constantly told that racism, xenophobia, and fascism contradict European values? The ideological composition of Ukraine's Maidan square mirrored Europe. That's why so many in the West turned away from that mirror in horror.

For Oleksiy, Europe's discomfort at watching Ukraine resembled Caliban's grimace upon seeing the reflection of his own face.

"They say they're nationalists, but they're Nazis," the teenaged Roman Ratushnyy said of Svoboda, who for a time controlled City Hall. For Roman City Hall became a bad place: Svoboda—he told me—had turned it into a torture site where they used tear gas and beat captured policemen and *titushki*. Twenty-five-year-old Natalia Neshevets, Oleksiy Radynski's colleague at the Visual Culture Research Center, had introduced me to Taras and Roman Ratushnyy. During the first days of Euromaidan in November, Natalia and her friends had been targets of the far Right's aggression: their feminist posters were destroyed; sometimes they were attacked with tear gas. After 30 November, the small groups of those she called "Nazis" remained the same—Natalia explained—but their presence was less conspicuous: if they were about 10 percent of the people on the Maidan in November, she guessed they were about 1 percent in December. They were there the whole time, but they comprised a very small group.

"It's difficult to talk about," Natalia said.

Sławomir Sierakowski, the left-wing activist from Poland, defended the presence of nationalists—unlike his leftist Ukrainian friends like Oleksiy, who reacted with distaste to the slogan "Glory to Ukraine!" The phrase no longer had the exclusively nationalist meaning it once had, Sławomir argued. His friends disagreed; they rejected the slogan. Nonetheless these young people of the Left took a courageous part in the Maidan throughout—and stayed until the very end.

For Markiyan, Svoboda meant the bad guys; he suspected that some of Svoboda's members were Kremlin provocateurs, paid to create a pretext for propaganda claiming that the Maidan was full of fascists. The Russian American novelist Gary Shteyngart described Pravyi Sektor as "catnip to the newscasters" in Russia. Oleksiy pointed out that whether or not the members of Svoboda and Pravyi Sektor were literally paid provocateurs, while they might "subjectively" be Ukrainian nationalists, their existence was "objectively" serving the Kremlin. Had they not existed Putin would have had to invent them: in their absence, the Maidan might have engaged many more residents of eastern Ukraine—who suffered no less from Yanukovych's rule than anyone else, but who could be manipulated into believing that fascists from Galicia were coming to attack speakers of Russian.

In fact the division between Right and Left on the Maidan,

like the division between the Maidan and the "anti-Maidan," had little if anything to do with language. Yanukovych repeatedly warned Ukrainians that the Maidan was full of *Banderovtsy* who would persecute Russian-speakers and force them to speak only Ukrainian. Yet Russian, as much as Ukrainian, was the language of the Maidan.

It was on the Maidan, the philosopher Taras Dobko told me, that Russian became for him a language of freedom.

"It was my choice"

Ivan Vakarchuk the physicist was "a typical good father." Slava, in turn, was a good son. "We had classic paternalism," Slava described, "here is my father, he's always right, he's wise . . . he's like a good king." It was understood that his children should not oppose him, and Slava had no great desire to rebel.

"My father was always an unquestioned authority for me, like a hero," he said.

And like his father, Slava enrolled at Lviv University and completed his doctorate in physics. Then in 1998, just at the moment when his father hoped his oldest son would go to the United States to further his scientific career, Slava instead moved to Kiev to write songs.

The decision to abandon physics and move to the capital was "the boldest and most serious step in my life," Slava told me, "because music, not physics; because Kiev, not Lviv; because my desire, not my father's desire." His father, Slava knew, disagreed with his decision—but did not try to stop him. It was the moment in Slava's life that made all the difference; and for Slava, his father's granting him that freedom to choose his own life had a philosophical meaning still more important than Slava's fantastic success as a musician. Slava had made a decision to go to Kiev; his father had made a decision to respect his son's freedom.

"The value of personal freedom is a not a fundamental law of physics," Slava told students in London, "it's a choice."

"Choice" was a word I heard often. There were moments when Markiyan was certain the revolution had been lost. Yet he kept going back. Once someone asked why he was standing there freezing on the Maidan if he believed all was about to be lost? His only answer was that it was his choice.

Taras Dobko was a philosopher. For him the Maidan was a rare experience of authenticity in the deepest existentialist sense: making decisions and taking responsibility. This authenticity was born of *Grenzerfahrungen*, of "border experiences," and came at a high price. On Christmas Eve Volodymyr Sklokin, a young historian, attended services with his wife in the eastern Ukrainian city of Kharkiv. As they were walking out of the church they saw their friend Vasyl Riabok, one of the coordinators of the Kharkiv Maidan. Vasyl Riabok was pale and nervous; he did not say "Merry Christmas." Instead he told them that

Dmytro Pylypets, a fellow activist in Kharkiv, had been attacked; he had been beaten severely and stabbed several times. It was unclear whether he would survive.

"I think that it was in those hours," Volodymyr Sklokin recalled afterwards,

> that I experienced what at one time or another every participant in a revolution experiences. My reason said that resistance made no sense, that it would make more sense to await a better moment to change the regime. I asked myself what we could possibly do against a regime that controlled the militia and was willing to behave criminally. And what could we do in Kharkiv, where the opposition was supported by only about 30–40 percent of the population? My reason said: better not to do anything, better not to yield to those provocations. And then I asked myself how I would look in the eyes of Vasyl Riabok if I did not come to the meeting that day. How would we look to one another if we all gave up? And at that moment the most important argument became my realization that if I gave up then, I would no longer be myself, but someone else.

As the situation grew more and more dangerous, Ola Hnatiuk's husband would send anxious text messages from Warsaw. "Are you going?" he would ask her. And she had to decide: would she go back to the Maidan, or not? She went.

Ola could have gone home to Warsaw. Instead she stayed in Kiev. She was there on 16 January when Yanukovych, with an illegal show-of-hands vote in the parliament, forced the passage of "dictatorship laws" revoking parliamentarian immunity and the rights of free speech and assembly. For Taras Dobko it was on 16 January that the line was crossed: the complete absence of law meant that everyone was vulnerable, that no one had any protection from the government at all.

"I describe it by this Yiddish word *chutzpah*," he said to me, "the way the laws were passed and how they were presented, that was really shameless." Afterwards, he said, there was "a desperate feeling among people . . . how can we live in such a country?"

"Everyone understands," Ola wrote to me, "that this is an unequal battle . . . but if they go out on the streets, it's because they don't want to live in degradation." By virtue of the 16 January laws, everyone who had taken part in the Maidan was a criminal and could be arrested. Yet as he had on 30 November, now, too, Yanukovych miscalculated. After 16 January everyone understood that no one would be safe as long as Yanukovych remained in power. He had raised the stakes: now it was all or nothing.

"Nobody taught us how to make revolutions," Iryna Iaremko, the Lviv real estate agent, said to me. She and her fellow volunteers understood only that they needed to organize people and take them to Kiev. For one hundred hryvnias, about twelve dollars, they guaranteed round-trip transportation. Many women wanted to go as well, but they had a rule: they would take only men. Lviv's mayor was on their side; even so, it was conspiratorial work, involving an intricate division of labor. "Everyone knew his job," she repeated. They brought food, clothes, shoes, and other supplies to Kiev. They invented code words for the military equipment they smuggled to the Maidan, describing bulletproof vests as *"maechkiy,"* undershirts. In the other direction they smuggled the wounded back to Lviv. They had to rotate roles frequently among themselves, especially the role of the person receiving the men who were about to board the buses.

Those in Lviv who could not go themselves came to donate money. Students donated the pocket money they would have used for beer and cigarettes; elderly men and women donated money from their tiny pensions. Iryna and her colleagues asked the donors to write their names, the year of their birth, and the amount of money in a notebook. These were schoolchildren's notebooks, small and square, sometimes with graph paper instead of ruled lines; their soft covers often contained a white rectangle for the pupil's name amidst sundry tacky images. One cover pictured blue jeans framing a photograph of a cowboy from a Western, another pictured coffee beans in the shape of a heart. An eighty-eight-year-old man came with two thousand dollars.

"I won't take that," Iryna told him.

"I know what I'm doing," he insisted.

(This story she told in Ukrainian, and I understood her, although I had been asking her questions in Polish, and until then she had been answering me in Russian. My Bulgarian friend Ivan Krastev, when I told him about my conversation with Iryna Iaremko, considered this symbolic: in order to understand deeply multilingual Ukraine you should be ready to ask questions in one language and listen to the answers in another.)

Jurko Prochasko was in Kraków, in Poland, on 17 January when he learned from the Polish newspaper *Gazeta Wyborcza* what had just happened. He understood at once what it meant. And he began to feel sick: he realized that they were being forced to radicalize, that a "non-radical conversation is simply not possible with Yanukovych." The Ukrainian president had at his disposal not only the police, the military, and the special riot troops named Berkut, but also *titushki*, thugs-for-hire recruited among criminals and hooligans. Yanukovych's response to peaceful protests was increasingly ruthless: by this time Berkut was using tear gas, rubber bullets, flash-bang grenades, and water cannons in subfreezing temperatures. Activists were disappearing. Some returned, some did not. Those who returned were often maimed and disfigured, missing, for instance, part of an ear.

From Kraków Jurko went on to Vienna, and it was there that he learned of the first deaths in battle on Hrushevskyi Street: the Armenian Serhiy Nigoyan and the Belarusian Mikhail Zhiznevskii. This was the moment, Slava Vakarchuk believed, that changed people in his country: these first deaths instigated "the main tectonic shift . . . towards something more responsible and less paternalistic." For Jurko it felt unbearable to be in Vienna then: in Ukraine people were dying, and he was in Vienna. He wanted only one thing: to go home. He returned to Lviv just at the moment when the body of Yuri Verbitsky was found in the woods. On the Maidan fragments from a police stun grenade had blown into Verbitsky's eye. Another activist brought him to the hospital, and from the hospital both men were kidnapped, taken to a forest, and brutalized. Yuri Verbitsky's body, battered and frozen, was found the following day. Professor Verbitsky had never been a radical. He was a fifty-year-old geologist who researched tectonic movements of the earth.

Jurko began to prepare for a longer stay in Kiev. Everyone understood that in Lviv there was nothing to be done. The whole city, even the mayor, was on the side of the revolution, in Lviv "everything had already been won." There was a consensus: women and children should stay, but men should go to Kiev. It was not long after the Christian holiday of Epiphany, and Jurko's family was invited by his son's godmother's family for lunch. Their hosts had invited as well the godparents of their own children, who arrived in tears. This second godmother had once been Yuri Verbitsky's wife. They had divorced years earlier; she had remarried, he had not. The adults sent the children to play in another room; even so, Jurko's older son, at eleven years old, was too old not to understand. Yuri Verbitsky's funeral had taken place in Lviv just three days earlier.

"And when we come home," Jurko told me,

my older son, the one who painted the banner that first evening, comes to me with tears in his eyes and says, "Daddy, you have to promise me that you'll never again go to Kiev to the revolution. Tell me: yes or no." . . . . and I'm convinced that I have to do this, that I have to go, and who if not me and everyone together. But on the other hand a child is crying and looking into your eyes and waiting for an answer and saying, "Tell me that you will never, ever go there again." And I said, "Yes, I promise you, I won't go there anymore."

"It was my choice," Jurko told me. He knew people whose families pleaded with them not to go, but still they went. But he made this choice. It was not easy for him to accept afterwards.

Okay, so all the more did I go every day to the revolution here, to the small Maidan, but I knew this was trivial. Yes, it was important, I stood there in the freezing cold for hours and hours, but it was not the same thing as being in Kiev, where everything was radicalizing. . . . the whole time I felt guilty that I was here and not there. And the tension, I just lived in those thoughts and emotions, checking the news every three minutes . . . and in the awareness that you shouldn't be here, because you're a young, healthy man, and other young, healthy men are there.

Jurko knew it was not in his character to throw himself on the barricades, to shoot, to die as a hero. Yet even so, he knew that there was an enormous difference between being in Lviv and being in Kiev.

When Time Was Smashed

"We understood perfectly that we were not going back, only forward," Iryna Iaremko told me.

No one slept more than three or four hours a night. Sometimes Iryna forgot what day of the week it was, or what date in the month. Everyone began to lose track of time. Victoria Sereda, a sociologist in Lviv whose husband, Ostap, had introduced me to Iryna, conducted interviews with people on the Maidan. One was with a clarinetist from Russia who had moved to Kiev five years earlier. He had played on the Maidan with his klezmer ensemble a few times in December. When? Was it earlier in December or later? He could not remember. Time had become very blurry.

"You know," he said, "I absolutely don't remember, it feels strange to me now, what's happening with time."

"Time was smashed," Mariya Borysova described. This especially frustrated Pavlo Khazan, an environmental scientist from Dnipropetrovsk who had devoted his career to renewable energy. He was used to working with formulas, integrals, tensors; now he had difficulty narrating the exact chronology of events.

"I'm a physicist," he told me, as he struggled with the dates, "I like precision."

Time on the Maidan was different from time elsewhere; on the Maidan people experienced what physicists like Pavlo had tried to explain for the past century: that time and space were not really separate things, that they were bound up with each other. "And again I lost a sense of time," Misha Martynenko described at regular intervals, as he narrated his experiences. When we met in Lviv, Markiyan Prochasko tried to generate a chronology of his time in Kiev. Inside the café where we were sitting there was no cell phone reception, and again and again Markiyan ran outside in the rain, his ice cream melting in a bowl on the table, to call his girlfriend, to check the dates.

"It's worth remembering," wrote Markiyan's father, Taras Prochasko, "that in our country people drink a lot. . . . Vodka belongs to the basic elements of Ukrainian cosmogony. It's present all the time and everywhere." And so it was all the more striking that this vertiginous confusion about temporality came about in the absence of vodka: there was no alcohol on the Maidan. Discipline reigned; a certain austerity prevailed around the iron cauldrons. Misha Martynenko celebrated New Year's on the

Maidan and was stunned at the absence of drunkenness. By then something had shifted. In the beginning Euromaidan had borne some resemblance to the parking lot of a Grateful Dead concert: food, drinks, clothing, a piano, drums. By January the atmosphere had changed. Taras Dobko understood: "It's not carnival anymore."

That there was no alcohol was still more remarkable because of the cold. It was a piercing winter; often the temperature fell below zero degrees Fahrenheit. People spoke about "standing on the Maidan," but the historian Yaroslav Hrytsak pointed out that "to stand" was not the right verb, because in such temperatures standing was impossible. It was essential to keep moving. Misha Martynenko described to me how sometimes he and his friends got so cold that their lips froze and they could not talk. Yaroslav's wife, Olenka, added that they all smelled of smoke from the cauldrons and the bonfires.

For Slava Vakarchuk it was a new experience: not to be on stage. Ordinarily he could not walk a block in Kiev without being asked to pose for a photo. Now on the Maidan he was one of a crowd; rarely did anyone ask for a picture or an autograph. Being in the audience felt very good, he said, it felt much better than being on stage—where he did not especially want to be. The Maidan was "like a political Babylon, you never know who is next to you on the stage." So Slava tried to avoid it.

Slava was sociable by nature; he liked to meet people, to talk to them. And on the Maidan he spent his time talking to people—ordinary people and politicians, those on the Left and those on the Right. His younger brother, too, was there. So was Lialia, Slava's very beautiful wife. "She's a revolutionary," Slava said of Lialia, although she was not a public persona and did not enjoy being photographed or giving interviews. A stylist and fashion designer, Lialia spent her time on the Maidan helping at medical clinics, collecting warm clothing, preparing food. She was there as "a field person"—Slava described—"like a typical, ordinary soldier."

Such "ordinary soldiers" gave the Maidan its character. Katia Mishchenko's husband, Vasyl Cherepanyn, director of the Visual Culture Research Center, which played a central role in the Maidan's Open University, often stayed through the night.

"I don't believe in ritual politics, I only believe in corporeal politics," said Vasyl. It was important to have actual bodies there.

"The moment you were there," Slava told me, "you felt like what they called 'a drop in the ocean,' and you're a big ocean."

Each person was a pixel, explained Yaroslav Hrytsak, and pixels always functioned together. People moved in groups, formed spontaneously. One night Yaroslav found himself pacing the Maidan with a philosopher friend, a businessman acquaintance, and the businessman's companion that evening, "a tiny man with sad eyes" who worked as a professional clown for a charity benefitting children with cancer.

Opening oneself to clowns and other strangers was a special feat in conditions of provocation. Taras Prochasko once portrayed his country as an apple dangling on a string at a fair, where the game was to bite the apple without using one's hands. Ukraine was that which could not be grasped. Russian television spoke about "Gayropa." Yanukovych claimed to the Western media that the Maidan was filled with fascists and antisemites—while telling his own riot police that the Maidan was filled with gays and Jews. His regime orchestrated a provocation: they posted advertisements in social networks offering between one hundred and one hundred fifty euros for actors to stage a fake gay pride parade. Katia Mishchenko described how the "pseudo-activists" were dressed up to look exactly "as they must have looked in the homophobic imagination of the organizers of this campaign: garishly dressed hedonists who could hardly wait to brandish their flags and, as the propaganda so beautifully puts it, 'disparage the innocent, childlike symbol of the rainbow.'" The plan was twofold: first, to offend those on the Maidan who were more conservative. And second, to provoke fights, perhaps between the authentic LGBT activists and their caricatures, which could then be exploited for the benefit of Western media as evidence of fascist tendencies on the Maidan.

"Contemporary Ukraine is a postmodern country," wrote Taras Prochasko. "Everything is possible here."

To Katia Mishchenko, having constantly to count on the possibility of provocation was more or less like having to pinch herself every minute to make sure she was not dreaming. "The government constructed a horrific house of mirrors," she wrote.

"The militia is running around in the uniforms of city sanitation workers, Berkut units rampage through the streets together with hired criminals, secret service agents toss a Ukrainian flag around their shoulders and go to spy on the Maidan, looters impersonate Pravyi Sektor. Nothing was as it seemed." On the Maidan, "Don't fall prey to provocation" became a refrain.

Markiyan Prochasko visited an "anti-Maidan" gathering in support of Yanukovych. There he met mostly middle-aged women; some heard his Galician accent and joked that he must be a spy. One told Markiyan that they had all come voluntarily; another told him that they had come on government orders; and a third told him that they had come for the free food. Most of them seemed to be civil servants from outside of Kiev. Some believed that this was a pro-European gathering, because Yanukovych had ostensibly been leading a pro-European course before he abruptly declined to sign the association agreement. There was much confusion. To Markiyan they all looked sad.

Often anti-Maidan demonstrators wandered over to the Maidan—sometimes in the role of spies or provocateurs, sometimes in search of better food. Everyone seemed to agree that they were identifiable by their sad faces. Those from the anti-Maidan *looked different*, Ihor and Victoria told me. The young men who kept guard at the entrance points to the Maidan practiced "face control," Ihor explained, and the check was simply visual: not facial features, but rather facial expressions had become identity markers. For Aleksandra Azarkhina, a student from Crimea, the essence of the Maidan was exchanging smiles with strangers.

"In Kiev the atmosphere is fantastic," Sławomir Sierakowski wrote to me from the Maidan in December.

No one knew how long that atmosphere would last. Ukraine, Taras Prochasko wrote, existed as a certain shared understanding that "at any moment with no warning all principles can be changed." This was also the premise of revolution itself: at any moment everything could change. Markiyan described how the atmosphere on the Maidan could shift startlingly quickly. For Katia the logic of the Maidan was the logic of dreams: the impossible suddenly became possible. Temporality took on a new form. It was essential to act in real time, even as the present felt so fugitive as to be imperceptible. At any given moment the state of affairs that had been obtained five minutes earlier could mean nothing.

(On 11 September 2001 my aunt, who lived in lower Manhattan, had just dropped off her six-year-old daughter at school and was walking past the World Trade Center when she saw an airplane fly into one of the towers. She phoned her husband at his office several blocks away. He told her to hurry back and grab their child, and then run north. My aunt was reluctant: she could not simply take her daughter out of school. My uncle insisted. When I saw my aunt a few days later, she told me about that phone conversation in the moments before the twin towers collapsed: how she had been thinking that their daughter was a child, that she belonged in school, that she had to be educated. She could not absorb fast enough, she told me, that the world that had existed several minutes earlier was no more, that the rules of that former world were meaningless.)

Now in Kiev no one slept anymore, Katia could phone anyone at any hour of the day. Everyone feared falling asleep: after all, one could awaken in a few hours to learn that everything, absolutely everything, was different.

Automaidan

Shortly after the "dictatorship laws" were passed, the first injured protestors were kidnapped. Katia was in Kiev then. The *Afgantsy*, veterans of the Soviet war in Afghanistan, went to serve as guards in the hospital near her apartment, protecting patients from kidnappings. On 23 January at 3 in the morning Berkut headed to the hospital. The *Afgantsy* called the "Automaidan"—middle-class activists with cars—for help. When the Automaidan drivers arrived, they were immediately kidnapped themselves, just yards away from Katia's building. She watched it happen. She told her friends; her telephone did not stop ringing. The wife of one of the men called, her voice shaking. Katia did not know what to say.

One of the men whom Katia saw taken was Andriy Shmindiuk, an Automaidan driver who also liked to ride motorcycles.

He very much looked like a biker: a large man in his mid-thirties with a shaven head, a light moustache, a thick beard. He had grown up in western Ukraine, then as a young adult moved to Kiev where he became CEO of an IT company—and the owner of an expensive car. Now he joined the Automaidan—like all patriots who owned cars, he said. The drivers had various jobs: to keep watch at hospitals; to transport tires for building barricades; to drive members of *Samooborona*, the Maidan's self-defense units, to places where *titushki* were spotted; to take captured *titushki* to the Maidan for interrogation. The Automaidan had a rule, Andriy told me: no beating the *titushki*—although he did not exclude the possibility that this rule was sometimes broken. The protocol, though, was to photograph their identity documents. One way the *titushki* exposed themselves was by their lack of knowledge of Kiev: most of them were not from the capital.

Andriy and the other drivers communicated through the "Automaidan channel," a smartphone application that functioned like a CB radio.

That night Andriy was driving on Shchors Street, patrolling in the Pechersk district, when at 3 am the SOS call came from hospital no. 17 on Laboratorna Street. Andriy was among the dozen or so Automaidan drivers who arrived at the hospital within two or three minutes. The drivers got out of their cars and approached five young men standing outside. They asked for the men's identification and learned they were from Cher-kassy oblast, a few hours' drive away. What were they doing in the middle of the night in Kiev? They had come to visit their friend at the hospital, they said. At 3 am? Andriy did not believe them. It was late and dark, and he did not notice the Berkut buses. Then one of the other Automaidan drivers heard "*rabo-taem!*" This was police slang: *Let's get started!*

"It was a very cruel beating," Andriy told me, "I did not know it was possible in Ukraine."

Andriy and I were at a café in Kiev with Katia, who had in-troduced us. Andriy was not dressed like a CEO: he was wear-ing a t-shirt underneath a hooded sweatshirt. Nearly a year had passed since that night, and Andriy still needed to take expensive medication every day; he had suffered some brain damage, he told me, and could no longer work in his previous position.

Andriy believed that the *Berkutovtsy* had not been sober, that they had been given some kind of drug; their pupils seemed to him strangely large, as if they did not react normally to light. To Andriy they seemed insane. They beat everyone, including some *titushki* and ordinary policemen who were on the ground shouting "*svoi! svoi!*" *I'm one of you!* They beat the men on the skull; Andriy guessed he had taken more than 150 blows. His head was pummeled by plastic and metal clubs. The bones in his hand were shattered. The *Berkutovtsy* used the clubs to bash the cars as well.

It lasted for twenty, maybe thirty minutes. Then the drivers were pushed onto the floor of a Berkut bus, and beaten more. *"Where is your 'Glory to Ukraine' now?"* the Berkut officers asked them.

No one broke—Andriy insisted to me—no one begged for mercy.

The men were taken to a police station, where they were left lying outside on the snow. Andriy drifted in and out of consciousness. Someone took away his wallet, his identification, his keys, and his phone. The police station did not want the mutilated Automaidan drivers there; and so the Berkut officers put them into the bus again, this time on the metal frames beneath the seats, the officers having removed the actual seats to avoid staining them with blood. By now, Andriy believed, the *Berkutovtsy* had grown more sober and were slowly orienting themselves to the fact that they had captured not some thugs from Pravyi Sektor, but rather middle-class men with white-collar jobs, some with "very good documents." They headed to another police station, this one in the Darnytsia district. The men spoke very little to one another: it was not safe, they did not know who was who, who might be an informer or a provocateur. By the time they found themselves in the basement of the police station in Darnytsia it was around 4:30 am.

An hour later Andriy's fiancée, Dasha, arrived at the Darnytsia station. Dasha had been calling Andriy every twenty or thirty minutes during his patrol that night. When around 3 am he stopped answering his phone, she looked on the internet and found the SOS message about the hospital on Laboratorna Street. She took a cab; once she arrived at the hospital, people helped her follow the path of the Berkut bus. It was very, very cold. She waited outside the Darnytsia police station for hours; around 9 am she saw Andriy for a fleeting moment as he was taken away from the police station in handcuffs.

Andriy was brought to the hospital's prison wing, secured by barred windows and guards, one of whom Dasha bribed to let her inside. In the days that followed, Andriy heard rumors of attempts to negotiate a deal: the government would release captives in exchange for the return of occupied government buildings. At the time, the Maidan controlled Kiev's City Hall, as well as regional state administration buildings in other oblasts. In a note to his lawyers Andriy called on representatives of the Maidan not to yield to provocation, the government was not to be trusted.

"Ukraine is a strong-willed nation," he wrote. "We will not be forced to our knees! *Glory to Ukraine!*"

Dasha was a physician. She was also a biker, like Andriy; this was how they had met. Andriy was a large man; Dasha was much smaller, and a dozen years younger. She was beautiful in a classical way: thin, with long blond hair and straight bangs framing big eyes accented with thick mascara. She posted the notes she smuggled out for Andriy on her Facebook page. He wrote in Ukrainian; she wrote in Russian—messages to friends and a prayer for Andriy:

I myself am not a religious person. I know no prayers.
But today I plead with you, God: he's a good man, treat him with
care...
Sometimes, unafraid, he throws himself into the depths of rivers
Suddenly the waves surge—help him, God, take care of him.

Values

Andriy Shmindiuk was still imprisoned on 2 February when Yaroslav Hrytsak noted that, thanks to continual donations, the Maidan had unlimited supplies. "The spirit of protesters is very high," he wrote, "and the support from people in Kyiv is very strong." His own spirits, too, were high: he had long believed that Ukrainians were fixated on questions of identity when they should be focusing on values. The language of identity was Putin's language; to Yaroslav it was a trap. This revolution was a revolution of values. Slava Vakarchuk felt the same way: the imperative of the moment was to "think hard" about what they valued. Slava had long sensed that the fall of the Soviet Union recalled the Exodus: Ukrainians would have to wander for forty years in the desert, waiting until the old generation with the values of slaves had died out.

The condition for new values, Taras Dobko had written several years earlier, was Ukrainian society's "shaking itself out of moral blindness." It was not a simple task in a country so saturated with corruption that everyone seemed to be implicated. *Prodazhnost'* (in Russian; *prodazhnist'* in Ukrainian) meant literally "saleability" and was epidemic, taken as a given at all levels, from politicians and media moguls to physicians and teachers, to locksmiths and parking attendants.

"Everyone is used to it, it's become as if a norm," Serhiy Zhadan told me.

It was understood as a matter of course that people could be bought. It was said that those who stole only a little and those who stole a lot differed only trivially, by the accidental matter of degree. Taras Dobko pointed out that the government had long wanted it this way: if everyone was guilty of participation in an unjust system, then it appeared no one had a right to protest against injustice.

Yaroslav Hrytsak was a leftist unenchanted with nationalism. How to resist imperialism without succumbing to nationalism had long been a struggle, and not only for Ukrainians. For Yaroslav the Maidan was the place where a truly civic Ukrainian patriotism came into being. The history of Ukrainian-Jewish relations was a dark one. The Maidan opened a new chapter. The coming together of Ukrainians and Jews at a moment of revolution was a testimony to what Hannah Arendt described as "natality," a revelation of the human capacity to begin anew.

Mariya Borysova was a Jew who spoke Russian at home; whenever she was asked about her identity, she said "Ukrainian." In his first days as a commander of operations on the Maidan, Natan Khazin had said nothing about the fact that he was a Jew. Gradually he began to tell people.

"I was shocked by the reaction," he said. "People called me 'brother.' Everyone."

Natan Khazin's story was all the more striking given that both Yanukovych and Putin very much tried to "play the antisemitic card," as Lena Finberg described it. Leonid Finberg went further: he was certain that Yanukovych's accusing the protestors of antisemitism was part of a deliberate operation by the Russian secret services, designed to delegitimize the Maidan. Leonid threw his energy into countering the government propaganda: writing, publishing, giving interviews, defending their "Revolution of Dignity."

There were Jews on both sides, Leonid pointed out.

Yet not among their own friends, Lena added. They had lived in Kiev for a very long time, they knew many different people from many different circles, and everyone they knew was on the side of the Maidan.

"How do you feel as a Jew on the Maidan?" journalists asked Lena.

The question amused her: "The same way I feel as a Jew at the train station, at the seaside . . ."

"Well, how should I answer?" she laughed.

There was suddenly a feeling that not only ethnic divisions, but also socioeconomic divisions had been overcome. Katia Mishchenko pointed out that the homeless were integrated into the larger community for the first time. This even led to some amusing moments, Ola Hnatiuk wrote: in subfreezing temperatures, it was the homeless who were much more adept at pouring Molotov cocktails into bottles; they were the ones who could still use their fingers in the cold.

Violence tested values. Yanukovych had been responding to nonviolent protests with kidnappings and torture. More and more activists had disappeared. Their bodies had not been found. Berkut was using water cannons in temperatures far below freezing. They were stripping people naked in the ice and snow, cutting them with knives. A video clip that circled the internet showed Yanukovych's policemen tormenting a naked, frozen captive in the snow. Ski masks, called "balaclavas," came into fashion. At the cafés along the Maidan waiters and waitresses got used to the balaclavas. It suddenly became normal to see people with crowbars and baseball bats eating in sushi bars. A joke began circulating: a man in a balaclava wearing a helmet and carrying a baseball bat walks into a café. Who is he? The answer: you can be fairly certain that he speaks at least three languages, has completed two university degrees, and has a well-paying job. Misha Martynenko, bookish and very thin, acquired a helmet, a medical mask, and protective eye gear. The only winter coat he owned was red, and because he did not want to draw attention to himself, he instead put on six or seven sweaters, looking a bit—he described himself—like a teddy bear wearing a helmet.

Katia was spending days and nights at the hospital, guarding patients against being kidnapped. The political opposition leader Vitali Klitschko, a wealthy onetime boxing champion, had supported the revolution from the beginning. In early February Katia wondered aloud: "Why can't Klitschko buy a tank for the Maidan?"

One night, from his room in a hotel overlooking the Maidan, the journalist Taras Ratushnyy phoned his teenage son, Roman, who reassured his father: he was about to go home. They hung up. Moments later Taras saw Roman on the television news: he was calling on people to be calm, announcing that he and others were about to storm a building named the Ukrainian House. Taras, furious, ran outside and grabbed Roman. It was the second time something like that had happened, the second time Taras had pulled his son away. Even so, Roman was soon injured again by one of Berkut's grenades.

Throughout the winter, Slava Vakarchuk sought out members of Pravyi Sektor and Svoboda and tried to persuade them not to be the first to use violence. Slava knew, though, that if confronted with violence by the other side, people needed to defend themselves. On the Maidan he sensed the change in consciousness; he felt how the collective preparation for violence at first increased gradually "day by day by day," then began "soaring, exponentially." Slava, the physicist-turned-rock-star, used the analogy of cold water being gradually heated: initially there are no bubbles, no noticeable changes. Nonetheless the temperature rises, and eventually the water boils.

I asked Mariya Borysova's father how he felt about violence.

"Speaking purely as a man, I was very much in favor," Maksim answered. He knew, intellectually, that violence was a bad thing. But his heart very much wanted it.

"You've been psychologically prepared for revolution since childhood," I said to Jurko. "This constant waiting for the real revolution, the faith that some day the authentic revolution would come . . ."

"Here I have to say that I'm abnormal, because I told you how I grew up with the wholly narcissistic conviction that I was different from other people . . . and the version of revolution corresponding to my psychological preparation appeared as if it were to make itself. And if it were not to make itself, then it should somehow be made in a liberal way—without shooting, without killing anyone," Jurko answered, "—yet it turned out that not this time. Not this time."

The Very Atmosphere
Had Some Qualities

Tuesday 18 February 2014 was the twelfth day of the Sochi Winter Olympics. It was Putin's grand performance; he was hosting the world. In Kiev it was almost spring. The temperature was over forty degrees Fahrenheit that morning when protestors on the Maidan marched to the parliament demanding the restoration of the 2004 constitution, which had limited the powers of the president. Outside the parliament building, Yanukovych's militia used stun grenades, tear gas, truncheons, and rubber bullets to chase back the crowd. An iconic photograph appeared on the internet: a fifty-nine-year-old father and his twenty-seven-year-old son, Mykola and Ihor Kuznetsov, their hair soaked in blood and their faces dripping red. *Berkutovtsy* began to arrive en masse; on the Maidan people used fires to keep them at a distance. Kievans separated into two groups: those fleeing the center and those streaming towards it.

Yanukovych issued a warning: leave the streets before six o'clock in the evening. He shut down the metro. Taxi companies refused to pick up passengers. Mariya Borysova noticed that something "felt weird."

"The very atmosphere—it had some qualities," Taras Dobko told me.

That morning Lena Finberg, who was seeing patients at her clinic, checked Facebook and saw the call for doctors to come to the Maidan right away. Lena, limping, began to run.

And I'm running to Khreshchatyk Street, along Bessarabka—which is close, but on Bessarabka shops are open, cafés are open—and I don't understand. I'm thinking that it must be some kind of a hoax: I don't understand how it can be that over there people are shooting while here a different, peaceful life is going on. Then the closer I came to Khreshchatyk, the fewer shops were open, everything was closing. And when I arrived, there were already people killed and wounded, and very few doctors. And everyone who came got to work right away.

Inside the Trade Union building there were long corridors filled with chairs, and in each chair a patient was being treated by a doctor. Two offices were being used for the wounded who were too weak to sit and had to lie down. Seeping into the building was the gas Berkut was using against the Maidan. Inside the doctors were sneezing and coughing, their eyes tearing as they treated the patients. From time to time someone would come and wash out their noses and eyes. The doctors all wore medical masks; they could not see one another's faces. More and more wounded were brought in. Berkut was using stun grenades. The shards caused gruesome wounds; the blood and the swelling were horrific. Lena and the other doctors cleaned the wounds and removed the fine pieces of metal.

In the same corridor, on inflatable mattresses, lay the bodies of those who no longer needed help.

No one spoke.

Late in the morning Lena looked out the window and saw that Khreshchatyk Street, Kiev's main shopping boulevard, together with the whole Maidan was lit up, as if it were all a scene from the theater. To Lena it seemed unreal. As Berkut's forces approached the Trade Union Building, the director of the medical services ordered all the women to leave and to take with them the wounded. Outside Automaidan drivers awaited them. One of the drivers took Lena and two patients to an underground clinic; the public hospitals were not safe. By now the Maidan had its own network of medical clinics, housed, for instance, in expensive boutiques. They drove to a dental clinic that had been converted into an emergency room. Men with shields surrounded the building.

"They must be ours," Lena told the driver when she saw the armed men.

"No," he said, "they're not ours."

He veered his car onto the sidewalk, switched course, and sped them off to another part of the city. Only later did Lena appreciate that the men with shields were *titushki* and that the Automaidan driver had saved her and her patients.

For Lena there was never a question of what to do: she was a doctor and people were wounded. She got to work.

I asked Lena if she had been afraid.

"Usually I'm such a coward," she said, "but at that moment there was no fear at all."

As soon as she arrived home, she turned on the television. Then the fear came.

"It was horrible. I started to tremble and then I really did become afraid. I started shaking all over."

Nelia Vakhovska had never liked the slogan "glory to Ukraine—glory to the heroes!" To her it stood for "empty discourse about a nation, machismo, paramilitary discipline, the unruliness of radical right-wing groups, the absence of a political or social programme." Revolutions were populist by their nature; they strove for the reduction of complexity. Nelia did not like this either. She feared the glorification of victimhood, the cult of heroes and martyrs. Even so, she was continually drawn back to the Maidan.

"On days like today," she wrote on 18 February, ". . . ideological incompatibility goes out the window and I take the side of citizens in conflict with their state. From this point of impotent rage, I repeat: 'Don't shoot, you bastards!' And I go to help at the hospital."

Mariya Borysova went to volunteer at a medical station, where she was put to work sorting medicines. Everyone was looking for a way to do something, so as not to do nothing. Yustyna Kravchuk described "a whole industry of Molotov cocktail production, mostly women." When someone said, "Let's go build another barricade," Taras Dobko told me, people responded like ants: they began building, often in silence. They dug up bricks from the street to crush and pack. Mariya's father, Maksim, was among those building barricades. Roman Ratushnyy's father, Taras, was as well.

"Isn't it hard to crush a brick?" I asked Taras Ratushnyy.

"With another brick?"

He had not found it so difficult. Petite Ola Hnatiuk, who dressed in elegant, tailored clothes and expressed herself in refined literary language, had also been smashing bricks that winter. It was something she never would have expected of herself.

"By now our situation has exceeded the boundaries of any kind of rationalism," Taras Prochasko wrote that night of 18 February. "Even basic self-preservation instincts are not functioning."

The Nonanalytical Point

In physics, Slava explained, there was something called a "non-analytical point": the point where all existing means of rational calculation break down. On 18 February the Maidan reached the nonanalytical point. A critical mass had made a decision: they would die there if need be.

Some of Vasyl Cherepanyn's friends told him to go home: he was a father, his daughter was ten years old. Vasyl stayed.

"Did your daughter know you were there when people were being shot?" I asked him.

"Yes, I think she knew."

Misha Martynenko had a younger sister the same age as Vasyl's daughter. Misha was the only man in the household: his father had left the family when he was three; Misha had been raised by his mother and grandmother in an apartment a few miles from the Maidan, across the Dnipro river on the Left Bank. Many people depended on him: his mother, grandmother, and sister; his teenage students at a local secondary school; his friend Zhenia, who was intellectually gifted but nearly blind. Zhenia had already finished one higher degree in music; now, with Misha's help, he was studying history. A subculture of reconstruction enthusiasts had developed in recent years; Zhenia was interested in reconstructions of World War II battles.

Misha looked frail, as if undernourished. There was a caramel glint in his dark brown eyes. As an infant he had been baptized in the Russian Orthodox Church; as a teenager Misha had chosen Greek Catholicism. When he awoke at 6 am on Tuesday 18 February, he put a white beaded cross around his neck. He ate breakfast very quietly, so as not to wake anyone. Nonetheless his mother appeared; she saw him getting ready to leave, and asked him to come back quickly.

"I'll be back by lunchtime," he told her.

Misha was a university student who wanted to become a historian of the Holocaust; he had no experience in the military. And he had never fired a gun. When he arrived on the Maidan that morning he joined those digging up paving stones to build barricades. He had gloves in his backpack, but forgot about them; his hands soon turned black. He saw an older historian whom he knew, a museum curator, who felt the escalating violence and made the decision to go home; he offered to take Misha with him. Misha thanked him for the offer and promised he would think about it—but he already knew he would stay.

Misha's friend Anton called.

"Where are you?" asked Anton.

"I'm there," Misha answered.

"I'm just leaving the university, I'll be there in thirty or forty minutes," Anton said.

Misha saw that *Samooborona* had taken some *titushki* prisoner. He did not feel sorry for the *titushki*.

He encountered a small Roma boy, not yet even adolescent, throwing rocks at the police. Misha told him to leave; it was dangerous, and he was just a child. But the boy was proud of his role, and told Misha that he had already thrown fifteen or twenty rocks. Misha began to take rocks in his hand and throw them himself; he would throw one, then run away from the grenade that came in response, then come back and throw another, then run away, then come back and throw another. Throwing the stones gave him a strange feeling of gaiety. He even began to laugh.

Misha did not know that some dozen people had already been killed. At that moment being on the Maidan was paradoxically like being in an informational vacuum: Misha did not even know what was happening a few hundred feet away. The internet connection was often weak; in any case there was no time to check the phone, Misha saw only what was right in front of him.

Misha's friend Anton arrived; they drank tea and smoked cigarettes. Before the Maidan Misha had been a casual smoker. Now he smoked constantly; it was the only thing that calmed him. Instytutska Street led from the Maidan up a hill; Misha and Anton decided to go there. Although it was still early in the day, Instytutska was already filled with more blood than Misha had ever seen before. He and Anton began screaming for medics to come, for people to make a corridor so that the medics could reach the wounded. When a car did manage to get through, it returned carrying two or three bodies covered with a blanket, and Misha understood that these were the bodies of the dead. On a pair of legs sticking out from under the blanket Misha saw a woman's high-heeled boots. *They were killing women.* That was the first moment when Misha understood that he might never come home.

A priest tried to negotiate with the militia, to implore them not to shoot. When the priest returned with his hands covering his face, Misha knew he had failed. The militia was shooting; Misha and Anton were throwing stones and running away, again and again. A grenade exploded so close to Misha's head that he was deafened. He was afraid, but less of death itself than of being taken captive and tortured. He was a student of history, and he knew that human beings were very inventive when it came to torture. Still he kept throwing stones; he had no other weapons; he and Anton and others fighting with them waited for reinforcements, but none appeared. Some of the *Samoobo-*

rona units seemed to be deserting. *Berkutovtsy* broke through the barricades and attacked. They looked to Misha like a *spetsnaz*, a tactical assault unit, and Misha and Anton had only the rocks, no real weapons.

"Look at me," Misha said to me when he told this story. "I'm not the kind of fighter to take on a *spetsnaz.*"

"We have to get out of here. Fast!" Misha shouted to Anton. They ran. As they were running, they heard a cry and saw a wounded man in civilian clothes; he was perhaps twice their age and much larger and heavier than either one of them.

"What's wrong?" Misha asked the man.

"I can't stand up. I can't walk."

"We'll carry him," Misha said to Anton.

They put the man on their shoulders, Misha turned around and saw that the militia men were only fifteen or twenty yards away, and they had to run.

"As I've already told you," he said to me, "I'm not very strong."

Anton was not much stronger. They went headlong down a steep decline; the ground was wet, they kept falling in the mud; their clothes were covered in sludge. Everyone else had run away, behind the barricade, and he and Anton and the injured stranger were alone on the hill that had become a no-man's-land. The militia were throwing grenades towards them. They had almost reached the barricade when Anton screamed, as if in a voice not his own, "Get down!"

The first shot came at them. Then came the second shot, and

Misha felt then that nothing mattered to him anymore, "as if I had removed myself. Such a strange sensation, as if nothing remained in my head, as if there were no more thoughts. It was not that my whole life passed before my eyes—no. It was as if there were nothing, nothing at all, no fear and also no courage. Nothing."

Then Misha saw the gunman reloading; it was the moment to escape, they were unlikely to survive another round of bullets. The man they carried was screaming; his wounded leg was dangling. Finally they reached the barricade, where they passed the man to the medical workers. Suddenly many people were congratulating Misha and Anton, strangers were looking at them as if they were heroes, or resurrected corpses, or both.

Misha and Anton said nothing at all; they walked away to smoke cigarettes.

A young man in a balaclava was staring at Misha, as if trying to make out his face. Misha took off his helmet—by now he felt warm—and it was then that the young man came up to him and said, "Glory to Ukraine!" Now Misha recognized Igor, his classmate. They were not friends. Igor was a member of Svoboda; he was a nationalist and an antisemite. More than once they had fought at the university, when Igor had said derogatory things about Jews and called them "*Zhidy,*" meaning "Kikes" or "Yids." He called Misha "*Zhid*" as well, although not because Misha had one Jewish grandfather—Igor had no way of knowing this—but rather because everyone knew that Misha was studying Jewish history and that he volunteered at the Ukrainian Center for Holocaust Studies. And so they hated each other.

Now, though, Igor was terribly happy to see him, and Misha felt that nothing about this happiness was false. Misha was the last person he had expected to see there at this moment, Igor told him. Some members of his Svoboda *sotnia*, the fighting unit Igor belonged to, had already deserted, but Igor was determined to stay on the Maidan and fight. He advised Misha to keep his face covered so that later he would not be identified in the militia's photographs.

Anton's mother called to say she was coming to join them, and Anton pleaded with Misha not to tell her what had happened, how close they had just come to being killed. By then it was nearly evening; the entire metro was shut down for the first time since the end of the Soviet Union. The city was paralyzed. Zhenia, Misha's friend who could barely see, called to tell them of Yanukovych's ultimatum: leave the Maidan by 6 pm or be considered a terrorist.

"There was no longer any way back," Misha said.

Around 5 pm their friend Grigorii, wearing a balaclava and carrying a small truncheon, joined Misha and Anton. They were told that volunteers were needed to evacuate the Ukrainian House, which had been serving as a medical center. First they carried out medicines and gas masks and other medical equipment. Then they carried out documents, and a package of passports.

"What should I do with them?" Misha asked a member of *Samooborona.*

"Burn them."

"How?"

"Douse them with the Molotov cocktail and set them on fire."

Misha did it; the passports dissolved in flames. It seemed the safest thing to do.

Two weeks earlier, while he and Zhenia were on a trip to Lviv, Misha had secretly fallen in love with a girl there named Maria, a Greek Catholic student at the university who believed deeply in God. She was very petite; Misha seemed tall next to her.

Now he looked at his phone and saw that Maria had called him several times.

"Misha, where are you?" she asked him.

"I'm there," he told her.

It was five minutes before six.

"In two hours I'll no longer be alive." He said this calmly, as if detachedly.

"I'll pray for you," she told him.

"Thank you."

"*Adieu.*"

"*Adieu.*"

Then Misha's mother called.

"Misha, come home!"

"Mama, I can't come home."

His grandmother called as well. Misha felt sorry for them, but . . . it was not easy for him, either. He could not come home.

It was close to 7 pm when the real attack began. The numbers of the wounded and the dying were ever greater; the police blocked the entrances to the Maidan and did not let the ambulances pass. Misha, Anton, and Grigorii, together with several others, some from *Samooborona*, decided to try to destroy one police blockade to open a corridor for the ambulances. Misha took a long stick. The men from *Samooborona* distributed Molotov cocktails. Misha had never killed anyone before, but now he felt that if he could strike one of the gunmen once, no one would be able to stop him. He had changed since that morning, having seen so much blood in so little time, having seen the legs with the high-heeled boots sticking out of the blanket, the militia stopping the doctors from saving the dying. It was inhuman.

"And it was as if, because of that, in me, too, there remained nothing human," he told me. He took the stick and thought, *"That's it. No mercy."*

Misha and his friends finished their cigarettes and covered their faces.

"Group, onward!" said the *Samooborona* commander. "Who has a lighter?"

Misha was dumbfounded: the man who was supposed to be the commander did not even have a lighter, the most basic thing.

"I have a good one," said Misha.

"Stay next to me. When I give the order, light my Molotov cocktail first, then the other ones."

The group approached the blockade.

"Light!" the *Samooborona* commander said to Misha.

Misha struck the lighter. Then he heard a voice booming through a megaphone, "One more step and we shoot to kill!"

Eight men drew their pistols and aimed at Misha's group. Misha and his friends stood as if dug into the ground. The *Samooborona* commander walked a bit further with his lit Molotov cocktail and then stood still as well. For the second time that day Misha experienced an absolute emptying of his mind. Once again, nothing was there. He recalled no scenes from his life. Even the hatred he had just felt disappeared. There was no fear and no bravery, there was simply nothing.

Then others came running. The intersection where they were standing had been empty, but now people—a few hundred of them—began to gather and shout at the police officers. "*How can you? How can you aim your guns at people?*" They started to film and take photographs. They started to threaten the police, "*If you start shooting them, we'll tear you apart!*" They made a line between Misha's group and the police officers; the *Samooborona* commander extinguished his Molotov cocktail, he did not want any civilian victims.

The policemen seemed taken aback, as if actually afraid; they put down their guns, got in their cars, and drove away. In the following hours, Misha and the others ploughed a corridor for the ambulances. Afterwards they went to find Anton's mother, who was waiting at a nearby café, where there were no other customers. Since they were still alive, they ordered tea. And they listened to the sounds of the sirens coming from the ambulances now able to evacuate the wounded.

It was close to midnight when Misha, Anton, and Grigorii, all too weak to do more, decided to go home. The metro was still closed; taxi drivers were asking for two or three times the usual fare. Finally they found a driver who would take them for a fair price; they paid him the last of their university stipends.

At home, on the other side of the Dnipro River, Misha could still hear the grenades and the gunshots. He knew the Maidan could not hold out; he expected arrests and purges to follow.

"Mama," Misha told his mother, "don't be surprised if they come for me."

The Buses from Lviv

That night of 18 February Slava Vakarchuk went to the Intercontinental Hotel for a meeting that lasted late into the night. Afterwards, Slava wanted to go home, but the hotel bodyguards would not let him leave: there was shooting on the street just outside the hotel. Slava looked through the Intercontinental's glass doors.

First he heard the shots.

"Then I saw the guy falling down," he told me.

The next day Slava learned that the man he had seen killed was a journalist. It was a strange thing—Slava described—to be at this five-star hotel with a spa and a swimming pool, with foreigners, with an expensive restaurant and bar, with life going on inside, and just outside the doors people are killing one another.

While Slava was looking through the glass doors of the Intercontinental, in Lviv Iryna Iaremko was loading buses. In the following hours she sent twenty buses of men to Kiev. Some had already been there, where they had been beaten or mauled by water cannons. They had returned home to recover; then they left for Kiev again.

"The boys were absolutely prepared to die," Iryna told me, "they absolutely understood where they were going."

I asked her about the women who stayed behind in Lviv, who must have been distraught about the men who said goodbye to them and boarded the buses.

No, she insisted, they were not distraught. "You know, it was pride. They were proud that their husband, their son . . . it was pride."

Misha Martynenko woke up that morning in the same mud-caked clothing he had fallen asleep in some ten hours before. He knew that the Maidan stood little chance of holding out against well-armed specially trained forces. And he understood that he and his friends would likely be killed; what mattered now was making the aggressors pay a high price for their deaths.

When Misha first opened his eyes that morning, he thought it might all be over. He checked the news: the Maidan was still standing.

Berkut was using real bullets; there were snipers on rooftops. Whole buildings were in flames. The Trade Union Building had been burning all night. That Wednesday morning many who were fighting there believed that this was end. Then they saw the buses arriving from Lviv.

Corpses

Serhiy Zhadan's novel *Voroshilovgrad* opens with the line, "Telephones exist in order to inform people of various unpleasant things."

Bohdan Solchanyk—who on 21 November had told his students that they could not make a revolution in one day—was on one of the buses arriving from Lviv. At twenty-eight years old, Bohdan held a lectureship in history at the Ukrainian Catholic University where Markiyan Prochasko and Maria, the girl with whom Misha had fallen in love, were students; where Yaroslav Hrytsak was a professor; and where Taras Dobko was vice-rector. On Thursday 20 February, Bohdan was on the Maidan with his friend Pavlo Salo when they got separated. Not long afterwards Pavlo came upon bodies that had been piled in front of a McDonald's. One of them belonged to Bohdan.

Pavlo took his friend's phone; he saw that Bohdan's fiancée, Marichka, had called seventeen times. Pavlo knew he had to call her.

Markiyan and his girlfriend knew Marichka. And Markiyan felt guilty that he had not died there on the Maidan together with Bohdan Solchanyk. Yet it was Bohdan's death that made Markiyan realize how much he wanted to live. He wanted to become a journalist and do something useful for Ukraine. He wanted to marry his girlfriend. He hoped they would have two children—both girls.

The Solidarity of the Shaken

"*We stand at the border/we reach out our arms,*" the former dissident Adam Michnik quoted the Polish poet Zbigniew Herbert. Adam was writing from Warsaw on Thursday 20 February: "Together with all of Poland, I repeat today: 'for our freedom and yours.' We send our Ukrainian brothers words of solidarity."

That day the young Ukrainian activist Aleksandra Kovaleva posted on Facebook an open letter to European politicians. "Yanukovych fucks you all this time, he fucks us also, but we at least are trying to resist," she wrote. "You're too old, you're blind to see what is happening, you are deaf and can not hear the screams." It was a *cri de coeur.*

"Sorry for my English," Kovaleva ended her letter.

Then she added, "And yes, thank you, Poland. We hear you and we love you."

Polish-Ukrainian solidarity could not be taken for granted. Poles and Ukrainians had fought a war in 1918. In 1943, during the Nazi occupation, militants of the Ukrainian Insurgent Army herded Poles into churches and set the churches on fire. They shot Poles and beat them to death with farm tools. There were hangings and decapitations. Poles responded, sometimes in kind. All together, some 50,000 Poles and 10,000 Ukrainians fell victim to the mutual ethnic cleansings. After the war, the Polish government, finding concentrations of ethnic Ukrainians inside Polish territory undesirable, removed by force some 141,000 Ukrainians from their homes and "resettled" them, dispersing them throughout the newly acquired territories of western Poland.

Now many wounded on the Maidan were taken across Ukraine's western border for medical treatment in Poland. In Vienna the left-wing weekly wrote, sympathetically if somewhat patronizingly, about "the kids from Kiev." The Polish press used the word "*powstańcy*" to describe those fighting on the Maidan. *Powstańcy*—those who rise up, resistance fighters—was a special word in Polish, surrounded by an almost religious sanctity; it was reserved for those who fought, as the nineteenth-century Polish insurrectionary slogan went, "for our freedom and yours."

All of the Polish insurrections of the nineteenth century failed. A century after the age of Romanticism, on 1 August 1944, the Polish underground in Warsaw once more rose up "for our freedom and yours," this time against Hitler's army. And once more, the uprising failed: the Germans burned Warsaw to the ground. A few months later, Stalin's Red Army crossed the Vistula River and occupied the ruins. Afterwards the communist regime rebuilt the Polish capital in Stalinist architecture. In 2014, the Palace of Culture, Stalin's monumental gift to the Poles, still towered in the center of Warsaw. When Kiev was burning, the city of Warsaw made the decision to light up the Palace of Culture in yellow and blue, the colors of the Ukrainian flag. It was a gesture that the Czech philosopher Jan Patočka would have called "the solidarity of the shaken." "The shaken" were those who had experienced descent into an abyss, an intimate encounter with mortality, "the transformation of the meaning of life which here trips on *nothingness*, on a boundary over which it cannot step, along which everything is transformed."

This was not the solidarity of those who had forgiven, or forgotten.

"The solidarity of the shaken," Patočka wrote, "is the solidarity of those who *understand*."

Andrzej Wajda's legendary film *Man of Iron* tells the story of the Polish students in March 1968 who go out into the streets to protest communist censorship and repression. One of those students goes home to his father, a shipyard worker in Gdansk, to ask for support. The father refuses. He strikes his son and locks him in his room. The moment is not right—the father insists; when the right moment comes, they will march together. *No!* vows the son from his locked room. *We will never march together.*

In Wajda's film, two years later during the December 1970 ship-yard strikes in Gdansk, it is the father who turns to his son. And the son responds in essence: you let us down two years ago, now you can go to hell. The father goes alone and is killed in the clashes at the shipyard. In these short scenes Andrzej Wajda captures the miracle of Poland's Solidarity movement born in the decade after those shipyard strikes: the coming together of not only the Right and the Left, and the Catholics and the Marxists, but also the workers and the intellectuals, the fathers and the sons.

For many veterans of Solidarity, the Maidan felt like the miracle they had never assumed they would live to see a second time. That overcoming of so many divisions lasted only for a moment, but it was a moment that most people never experienced. As in Poland in 1980, it belonged to what Hannah Arendt called "the treasure of revolution," "which, under the most varied circumstances, appears abruptly, unexpectedly, and disappears again, under different mysterious conditions, as though it were a fata morgana." It was a treasure, Arendt wrote, "beyond victory and defeat."

"Revolution is an event in the realm of the spirit," wrote Józef Tischner, the philosopher-priest who served as Solidarity's chaplain. "Each person has changed. In the new person, there is no trace of the clay from which were formed the former slave, vassal, work force. People cannot, even if they want to, regain their former shape. They now have different bones." In his role as a book editor, Leonid Finberg had published Hannah

Arendt's *Origins of Totalitarianism*. He published, too, a book of Adam Michnik's conversations with Tischner about Solidarity. Now Leonid distributed copies to activists on the Maidan: it seemed to him that what Adam Michnik and Józef Tischner were describing might have special meaning at this moment for Ukrainians.

In 2014 Eastern Europe was celebrating the quarter-century anniversary of communism's collapse. Former dissidents asked themselves: what happened to solidarity? It seemed to the Polish theater director Krzysztof Czyżewski that Poles had too easily assumed that the West had ready-made answers to all problems. The successful pursuit of individual freedom had left "the bitter taste of alienation, egoism and loneliness, as well as depression—the most common illness of liberal societies."

"We're dealing," wrote the Polish philosopher Marcin Król, another Solidarity veteran, "with a moderate economic crisis, a serious political crisis, a dramatic civilizational crisis and a perhaps fatal spiritual crisis."

"What is the fatal spiritual crisis?" a journalist asked.

"We've ceased posing questions to ourselves."

"What kind of questions?"

"Metaphysical questions. No one contemplates, for instance, where evil comes from."

Adam Michnik agreed. "This is a civilization that needs metaphysics," he told Václav Havel in 2003.

The Maidan was the return of metaphysics.

Burning Flesh

On Wednesday 19 February, after he had learned that the Maidan was still standing, Misha went to visit his friend Zhenia. Misha was very weak, his whole body hurt, he did not feel strong enough to go back. They watched video coverage of a tank burning.

"Misha, will you go there tomorrow?" asked Zhenia.

"If there is a where to go to, then yes."

"I'm going with you."

"Zhenia, relax! It's no place for you to be right now."

"Don't tell me what to do. I'm older than you are."

On Thursday morning there was still a where to go to—the Maidan was still standing. Misha called Zhenia around nine o'clock.

"Zhenia, you haven't changed your mind?"

"No."

"They're shooting there."

"I haven't changed my mind."

And so on Thursday morning Misha and Zhenia, who could barely see, went together to the Maidan. This time Misha did not even take a backpack, only a scarf to cover his face.

"If I told you I wasn't afraid," Misha said to me, "I would be lying."

They went to Instytutska Street to reinforce the barricades; they carried tires, and they joined a chain of men passing along stones. Women brought sandwiches; the men ate them as they worked.

Then someone screamed, "Sniper! Take cover!" And the chain of men dissolved; the men ran, hid, then returned. When they did, Misha asked an older man, a veteran of the war in Afghanistan who was reinforcing the barricade with him, what was going on, where the gunmen were hiding.

"You don't know?"

"We just got here an hour and a half ago. We don't know. We only know they've started shooting . . ."

"They've shot around a hundred people here."

There was a gendered division of labor: men were building barricades, women were making Molotov cocktails. Misha went to the women and offered to bring one of the boxes of Molotov cocktails to the front. As he carried the box he suddenly saw himself as if in the sniper's scope, the target of a gunman on a rooftop he could not see. Suddenly he was overcome with terror; he felt an impulse to drop the box of explosives and flee the Maidan. And he might have done that had not a stranger just at that moment offered to help carry the box. And Misha's terror dissolved as quickly as it had appeared.

In the city that day—Misha later learned from his mother—there was panic. Kievans waited in long lines to fill up their cars at gas stations, withdrew all the cash from the ATMs, emptied shelves at grocery stores. Misha's mother bought an axe.

On the Maidan itself the mood was very different: there was fear—Misha described—but not panic.

Later Misha returned to Instytutska Street to rejoin the chain reinforcing the barricades. He heard a shot, fifty or sixty yards away, and saw an unarmed man who had been shot in the neck fall to the ground.

Misha and Zhenia were joined by Zhenia's friend, a photographer who had just come from the now incinerated Trade Union House. The smell was hideous, the photographer said.

"What kind of smell?" Misha asked.

"Of burning flesh."

"You will all be dead"

Poles shared with Ukrainians something else as well: historical experience had taught them not to count on the West to save them from Russia. It was not a coincidence that on 19 February, as Kiev was burning, it was Polish foreign minister Radosław Sikorski who decided to go there.

On Thursday 20 February, mass shooting began around 8:30 in the morning. Oleksiy Radynski, the filmmaker, was at the Hotel Ukraina, watching the sniper massacre take place on Instytutska Street fourteen floors beneath him. Sikorski was making his way to the presidential palace. He had wanted to first visit the Maidan, but Yanukovych's men told him they could not guarantee his safety there—or the safety of his bodyguards.

Sikorski had met Yanukovych a few times before, and he believed that Yanukovych felt a bit of trust towards him. Yanukovych knew that Poland was Ukraine's main advocate in the European Union—and the government's official position was that Yanukovych had only postponed signing the association agreement and wanted to continue EU negotiations. Moreover, Sikorski was not among those enamored of Yulia Tymoshenko. On the previous occasions when Sikorski had spoken with Yanukovych, "I didn't harangue him about Yulia, he knew I wasn't a Yulia advocate."

When Sikorski and Yanukovych met that Thursday morning, the Maidan was burning. The presidential administration building on Bankova Street was only half a mile from the Maidan, and closer still to Instytutska Street. As Sikorski approached the palace, smoke wafted into the building. Yet once he was inside, the atmosphere was "strangely antiseptic."

Sikorski's decision to go to Kiev had the approval of Catherine Ashton, the European Union's High Representative for Foreign Affairs; German foreign minister Frank Walter Steinmeier and, briefly, French foreign minister Laurent Fabius joined him there. Together they represented the European Union. Putin sent the Russian Human Rights Commissioner, Vladimir Lukin, an older man and an experienced diplomat, whose creativity in overcoming impasses Sikorski appreciated.

"The main challenge," Sikorski said of Yanukovych, "was to get a word in edgewise, he would sit you down and talk at you."

Yanukovych was crafty; Sikorski was blunt. The things that Sikorski had expected to be difficult turned out to be strangely

easy: after a forty-five-minute phone call with Putin, Yanukovych agreed to shorten his presidential term and hold early
elections. He also agreed to bring back the 2004 constitution
limiting the president's powers.

Perhaps Putin had declined to give Yanukovych asylum in
Russia. Sikorski did not know what Putin had said during that
phone call.

At 5 that morning Slava Vakarchuk had gone back to the
Maidan. Around 6 am he headed home and went to sleep. A
few hours later he woke up "with a bad feeling" and called a
friend, who told him not to come to the Maidan because people
were being killed there. Instead they tried to lobby members of
parliament. When Slava arrived at the parliament at 12:30 or
1 pm, he could hear gunshots on the streets. Once inside and
through the checkpoints, he joined a few others who were im-
ploring members of parliament to stop the massacre. A line was
being crossed: if they did not stop now, they would be murderers. Slava and his friends were persuasive; the parliamentarians
passed a motion. The motion had no legal force, it was merely
symbolic; even so, Slava believed that the moral effect counted:
Yanukovych knew he was losing his parliamentary majority from
moment to moment, that his Party of Regions was splitting.

In the previous days, Yanukovych had summoned police and
Berkut regiments from around the country. Many came. Yet
ever more units, especially in western Ukraine, were defecting,
"crossing to the side of the people." Andriy Pavlyshyn, a trans-

lator of Polish literature, was among a crowd of activists in Lviv who rushed to the local Berkut headquarters to prevent the riot policemen from leaving for the capital. It was late in the evening and we were taking a slow walk through Lviv as Andriy told me this story. He was guiding me to historical sites from the 1939 to 1941 Soviet occupation: the editorial offices of an infamous Polish Stalinist newspaper, the restaurant where four Polish poets were arrested by the NKVD. I looked at him: a middle-aged man, a bit portly. It was difficult to imagine him winning a physical confrontation with a trained riot policeman—unless, of course, the riot policeman wanted to lose. Andriy had the same impression: the *Berkutovtsy* had tried to get out of the building— he told me—but they had not tried terribly hard.

While Misha and Zhenia were building barricades, and Misha's mother was purchasing an axe, Radosław Sikorski talked to Viktor Yanukovych. Yanukovych's security forces were conducting a massacre, yet the Ukrainian president maintained his "pretty stiff, Brezhnevite style." The Polish foreign minister knew that, as they spoke, more people were being killed. And he knew that the longer they talked, the more people would die. Yanukovych, though, did not show much emotion.

"He's not very bright," Sikorski told me later, "he doesn't have much imagination."

In the evening, the leaders of the opposition political parties —Vitali Klitschko of the Ukrainian Democratic Alliance for Reform, Oleh Tyahnybok of Svoboda, and Arseniy Yatseniuk of

Yulia Tymoshenko's All-Ukrainian Union "Fatherland"—joined them. While they had never controlled the Maidan, from the beginning the opposition leaders had taken its side. Now Sikorski noticed the lack of hostility between Klitschko, Yatseniuk, and Yanukovych; during the night they all drank vodka together, and the atmosphere of their negotiations was "remarkably untoxic." He was surprised, but not shocked.

Negotiations lasted all night. On Friday morning they had the text of an agreement: Yanukovych would hold a presidential election no later than December; until then, he would remain president. The shooting would stop. Klitschko and Yanukovych shook hands. Klitschko, though, failed to persuade the Maidan's representatives to sign the agreement. By then some 106 people had been killed, many by snipers. They were largely young men, often fathers, including a widowed single father leaving behind a three-year-old daughter. One was a sixty-one-year-old woman who had been a victim of Chernobyl; one a nineteen-year-old medalist in the 2013 Deaflympics; one an eighty-two-year-old man from Saint Petersburg who was a veteran of the Soviet navy; one a thirty-four-year-old anarchist from Crimea who had become friendly with Yustyna Kravchuk at the Visual Culture Research Center's film screenings.

Klitschko called Sikorski back to help.

"They've literally just seen their people die . . . so it was a very tough sell," Radosław Sikorski told me.

To the representatives of the Maidan, Sikorski made an emotional appeal: he had come of age in Poland during the Solidarity era. Solidarity was a miracle not unlike that of the Maidan: the overcoming of social divisions; a truly mass protest; a passionate insistence on moral values in the face of an immoral regime. In 1981—Sikorski told them—we underestimated the strength of the regime. We got martial law and mass internment. So agree to this now and then later ask for more, he advised.

The leaders of the Maidan were reluctant.

"If you don't support this," Sikorski finally said, "you will have martial law, the army, you will all be dead."

Pornographic Portraits

They signed—all but four of thirty-two.

An hour later Radosław Sikorski was on the Maidan. It was the moment of his greatest satisfaction: the shooting had stopped. The riot police dissolved into the landscape. The color, though, had not returned, and the novelist Yuri Andrukhovych was struck by how everything had turned black, full of ash and soot, as if everyone had just emerged from mines in the Donbas.

The sun had already set when twenty-six-year-old Volodymyr Parasiuk, breathless and unshaven, took the stage and spoke of those in his *sotnia* who had not survived. Klitschko stood on the stage as well, and the former boxer's face was somber, as if chiseled, as the crowd shouted together with Parasiuk, "*Shame! Shame!*" Volodymyr had come from Lviv together with his forty-nine-year-old father; the father and son had fought side by side on the barricades. While Volodymyr Parasiuk spoke, bodies of the dead were carried through the crowd in open coffins, and he called on the Maidan to accept no compromises with Yanukovych, a murderer.

Misha listened to Volodymyr Parasiuk, and he was on his side: Yanukovych had just ordered a massacre. He could not be allowed to remain president—not until December, not even for one more day. Misha watched the bodies being carried; he learned that Bohdan Solchanyk had been killed. And Misha thought to himself: "*Those beasts should not win.*"

"Mama," Misha said when he returned home, "tomorrow I'll go there again."

"What do you mean 'again'? How much can you do?"

"Mama, he cannot be allowed to stay."

"And what? You want to kill people?"

"Then I said to myself: '*Yes, Mama. If that's necessary, then I'm ready.*'"

In the end, it was not necessary. Radosław Sikorski had expected that this agreement would bring about the end of Yanukovych's regime, but he had imagined it would be a matter of weeks. As it turned out, it was a matter of hours. Yanukovych fled. Protestors stormed into his opulent residence in Mezhyhirya and found—amidst a boxing ring, antique automobiles, a private zoo with ostriches, and an exotic bird collection—a pornographic portrait of a naked Yanukovych and a loaf of bread made of gold. The protestors did not loot the villa; and Oleksiy

Radynski was unimpressed by how they exemplified "a bourgeois interest in the well-being of the upper classes rather than
a spirit of revolutionary destruction." Instead the thousands who
flooded to Mezhyhirya left the residence as it was, a kind of museum of an oligarch's tyranny—ostentation and absurdity.

On Saturday 22 February the Maidan was full. It was a beautiful day in Kiev, forty-eight degrees and sunny, unseasonably
warm. The *titushki* had disappeared. Shirtless men were playing
the drums. People read poetry on the stage. The parliament freed
Yulia Tymoshenko, who came directly to the Maidan, where,
seated in a wheelchair the color of wine, she was brought to the
microphone. Yulia, her golden hair still braided peasant-style,
had aged in prison.

"I am so proud of you," she said to the crowd, as if they were
her children.

There was something patronizing in her tone, Evita Peron
blended with Sarah Palin. She spoke to the crowd as if she had
freed them, and not they her.

The Revolutionary Soul

"Afterwards," Misha described, "I walked around like a somnambulist, like a zombie."

Misha was not the only one. After 21 February most people went home, but some stayed. They had lived for weeks amidst tear gas and police batons, water cannons and grenades. They had seen people killed before their eyes. Some had lost body parts, some had lost their sanity. A call was posted for psychotherapists to come to the Maidan. Jurko Prochasko went at once; it was his first opportunity to make up for not having been there during the past weeks. Now he spent the last nights of February in Kiev, approaching people who had lost their minds, trying to convince them they were not alone. Nobody slept. There was a feeling: this is a revolution, sleeping is impermissible. How could you sleep during a revolution?

Those wandering the Maidan were distraught. With Yanukovych's flight, the reign of revolutionary discipline had come to an end. Alcohol reappeared.

"They were saying, how is it possible," Jurko described, "how is it possible to drink alcohol? How nothing has ended yet. How at any moment danger could return. How is it possible to betray the memory of the fallen by drinking alcohol?"

Some of them were thinking of 2004, when everyone went home and Viktor Yushchenko betrayed them. *Not this time.* Not this time would those months of standing and freezing and being beaten be for nothing. This time they would stay until the revolution was implemented. And if the politicians did not implement the revolution's demands, then they would make another Maidan, and another one . . . They felt responsible to the dead, whom they had watched die. They felt responsible to them to remain there until they were certain the revolution was carried through to the end. There was a common feeling: the man who was drinking tea with me a few days ago is lying dead. If I leave this place, I will be betraying him.

Jurko's longest conversation lasted four hours. It was in Russian with an old man circling the Maidan with a club and a helmet, a former officer in the Soviet army who had been on the Maidan with the students from the very beginning, and who on 30 November had been beaten together with them. The night Jurko met him was the anniversary of those beatings. In December and January, on the last day of the month, there had been a mass on the Maidan in commemoration of that first act of brutality; it was always at 4 am, the time the attack had begun. Now it was the last day of February, and for the first time there was no mass. That man was running around the Maidan with his helmet and his club, looking for someone who could tell him where the mass was being held.

People like this elderly officer could not believe the revolution was over; they were unable to cease being revolutionaries.

"I didn't tell them that the revolution has ended, that you are heroes, that you're my heroes," Jurko said. He understood that in truth the revolution had not ended—and moreover, that such arguments would lead to nothing. Instead he told them: "Yes, that's true, the revolution has not ended, but please, go home, sleep, and afterwards you'll continue making the revolution."

For Jurko it was a moment of what Freud had called *Gegenübertragung*, or "countertransference": a feeling of rapture, of gratitude towards these people who were heroes for him, and at once a feeling as if a red light had come on, warning of danger to the psyche. It was an extraordinary experience. It was important to him as a psychotherapist: after all, when to be a psychotherapist if not precisely at this moment? It was important to him, too, because of his guilt for having stayed with his family in Lviv when people were being killed in Kiev. And it was important to him because it gave him insight into the revolutionary soul.

"Because I had understood everything," he told me.

I had understood that dynamic, why people want revolution, why they make a revolution, why they cannot do otherwise, why they devote themselves. I had understood dedication. But I had not understood one thing—for me this was the limit of my own experience—I had not understood the moment when a person is ready to die. And there I understood it. . . . it's a departure, a movement beyond the confines of the self, when you experience being with people who are ready to die for you, to make themselves vulnerable for you, to carry you if you're wounded . . . a willingness appears—it's a kind of rapture, a wonder at the possibilities given to man, an enormous gratitude towards others, simply a *Begeisterung* with generosity and devotion. And an experiencing of an enormous solidarity. . . . I don't know how much of this is Eros and how much is Thanatos, in any case, when a person is in such a state something appears that says that this experience of such enormous human solidarity is more important than the value of my individual life. And in such people the fear of death simply disappears, and there appears the conviction that because you are ready to die for me, I am ready to die for you. With no regrets. . . . of course this passes with time, but it passes only in those people in whom it appears. Because many people are not capable of such an experience. They don't go to the barricades. They hide, or they don't go in the first place . . . I'm not speaking about whether this is good or bad—that's not the question. The question is not whether this is extremism, or whether it's not extremism, or whether it would have been better to have kept the revolution nonviolent. This is simply phenomenological, it has to be understood, because otherwise we will have understood nothing about revolution. Nothing.

Dialectics of Transparency

"Revolution," wrote the Yugoslav philosopher Gajo Petrović, "should abolish self-alienation by creating truly human society and truly human man."

Like all revolutions, this one involved moments of radical contingency, when everything might have happened differently: if on 21 November Mustafa Nayyem had not written that short message on Facebook—"*Come on, let's be serious . . . 'likes' don't count*"—perhaps the Maidan would not have happened. The very sentence "'likes' don't count" would have made no sense before Facebook. It became a revolutionary slogan for the twenty-first century.

This was a revolution that began on Facebook and would have been impossible without it. Facebook and Twitter told friends and families who needed help, of what kind and where, who was harmed or unharmed, alive or dead. They were also the means by which the revolutionaries took control of their own narrative. Participants and sympathizers posted texts and videos on the internet, often with notes like "*Urgent! Maximize reposts!*" and "*Repost as many times as possible!*" Putin and Yanukovych won the propaganda war in the official media, but they lost in the social media.

The technology of social media had made possible a transparency that was unimaginable when Jurko and Taras Prochasko's and Taras Ratushnyy's generation took to the streets during the Gorbachev era. The technological revolution brought forth a situation Hegel described as a moment when quantitative changes became so great as to become qualitative changes, when changes in scale became changes in kind. The Maidan set up its own cameras; the Ukrainian revolution live-streamed *itself* on YouTube. Around the world everyone could watch Ukrainians being shot to death in real time.

Oleksiy Radynski was on the Maidan with his cameramen from the beginning to the end. He did not feel conspicuous: everyone seemed to be filming. Everyone had a camera, if only on a cellphone. At moments it was hard to find someone with two free hands. It was quite possible, it turned out, to throw a rock with one hand and film with the other. The essence of *proizvol* was to be rendered a plaything of authority's caprice, to be treated as an object, not a subject. The revolution against *proizvol* was an assertion of subjectivity, and for those on the

Maidan the possibility of transparency was a means of achieving subjectivity, of telling their own story.

"'*Subjectivity*,'" mused a Polish historian friend when we spoke about the Maidan. "I haven't thought about that word since the days of Solidarity."

In their desire to overcome the alienation of modernity, both democracy and totalitarianism, in their different ways, have long aspired to transparency: democracy to transparency of the government, totalitarianism to transparency of the private sphere. Yet the same transparency that promised perfect knowledge, a bridge from self to world, threatened the transgression of interiority. When the young paramedic Olesia Zhukovska, blood pouring from her neck, typed on her phone, "I am dying," her Twitter message traveled the globe in minutes. To strangers around the world, that message made Olesia Zhukovska a real person. At once that message robbed death of its intimacy; and this self-violation of intimacy became the means for the assertion of selfhood.

In Kiev, doctors performed emergency surgery; in the end, they saved Olesia. Yet a dialectic of transparency and subjectivity was no less present: the Maidan was the site of both the achievement and the violation, the fulfillment and the overcoming, of individual selfhood. The sacrifice was privacy.

"Without secrecy there is no friendship," Ivan Krastev said to me.

Chekhov's Gun

Taras Dobko feared that, after the revolution, the Maidan could become macabre. By mid-May, as the Ukrainian presidential election approached, it was no longer a moment of carnival, and no longer a moment of transcendence. On the Maidan there were still tents; the people living in them still cooked soup in iron cauldrons. No one was sure whether these were the same people who had been there all winter, who had no place else to go, or who were unable to face going home. Some wore camouflage. They were self-declared *Samooborona*; perhaps some of these were the same men who had belonged to *Samooborona* during the winter, perhaps not. The stage was still intact. In-stytutska Street, where many of the shootings had taken place between 18 and 21 February, wound uphill from the Maidan; the hill was covered with memorials, flowers, photographs of the dead, now referred to collectively as the *Nebesna Sotnia,* "the Heavenly Hundred."

Alongside the memorials I saw a man lying dead, face up on the sidewalk, blood across his face. A policewoman was photographing him. She was wearing a police officer's uniform with a very short skirt and extremely high heels. I doubted the scene was real. Perhaps the skirt could have been worn by a real policewoman, but not those heels. But I was wrong: the scene was real.

That night in Kiev I asked a Ukrainian colleague about the men in uniforms who remained on the Maidan, the ones who called themselves *Samooborona.* Something felt ominous there now.

Yes, some of them were armed, he told me, "and you know, for Chekhov . . ."

This was the feeling I had as well. The Russian writer Anton Chekhov took it to be a theatrical axiom that a gun, once visible on stage, be fired before the conclusion of the last act.

PART 2

War, East of Kiev

Russian Tourists

In spring of 2014 the Ukrainian Catholic University was organizing first-aid courses. Taras Dobko's students were volunteering for quasi-military training; a war to come might be a partisan one.

"There is a kind of understanding," Taras Dobko told me in April 2014, "that anything can happen."

A quarter-century after the fall of communism, this was a divide that remained between East and West: Western Europeans —like Americans—tended to believe, even if only subliminally, that there were constraints on reality, that borders would hold, that certain boundaries would not be crossed. Eastern Europeans knew that anything was possible.

During a conversation organized by a German newspaper in early February 2014, Jurko Prochasko had pointed out that

Ukrainian writers in the western part of the country were in a very different situation from those in the eastern part. In Galicia, everyone was on the side of the revolution. But Serhiy Zhadan, for instance—Jurko said—lived in Kharkiv, where most people did not support the Maidan. After the massacre in Kiev and Yanukovych's disappearance, the residents of Kharkiv remained divided. Russian "tourists" arrived from across the border to take part in "anti-Maidan" demonstrations. On 26 February, Serhiy Zhadan posted on YouTube, in both Russian and Ukrainian, a six-minute appeal to the residents of Kharkiv. Serhiy was a poet, a novelist, and a musician, but this video contained no poetry, no art, no music. His message was straightforward. He wore a black sweater, stood still, spoke directly into the camera.

Don't listen to the propaganda, he said. There are no Banderovtsy here. There are no fascists, no extremists. None of that is true. Come over to our side.

Three days later, on 1 March, Serhiy Zhadan was led away from a demonstration in Kharkiv bloodied, his head bashed in. He was taken to a hospital filled with the wounded from both sides. He approached a young man from the anti-Maidan crowd that had attacked him.

"His eyebrow was split open, he seemed confused," Serhiy recounted.

"How did you end up here?" I ask him.
"What does it mean 'how'? Out of principle."

"And why did you get into a fight?"

"I didn't want to. Suddenly things started up and there I was."

"Look out for yourself, there's really nothing that divides us," I say, and then we even hugged each other. I have no idea if he meant that seriously.

Jurko did not understand those who were against the revolution. He did not understand those living in the east who were full of fear and hatred towards the Maidan. He did not understand how they could be so susceptible to propaganda as to believe that people like Jurko were fascists who would descend upon them with weapons in hand and force them to speak Ukrainian and believe in Bandera. Jurko felt this to be a weakness in himself; he wanted to understand them.

Caligula at the Gates

"*Our respite was short-lived in the end,*" wrote the poet Tomas Venclova, the former Soviet dissident from Vilnius. In 1975, he had been one of the founders of the Lithuanian Helsinki Group created to monitor human rights. In 1977, he was forced to leave the Soviet Union. In 2014, he titled his poem about Vladimir Putin "Caligula at the Gates."

The Russian "tourists" who battered Serhiy Zhadan in Kharkiv ushered in the "Russian Spring." This began at the seaside, with the Russian annexation of the Black Sea peninsula called Crimea. "Little green men" in black masks and unmarked camouflage, who in fact were Russian special forces, appeared on the peninsula at the end of February. On 4 March Leonid Finberg was among the leaders of the Ukrainian Jewish community who signed an open letter to President Putin.

"Vladimir Vladimirovich," they wrote, "we highly value your concern about the safety and rights of Ukrainian national minorities. But we do not wish to be 'defended' by sundering Ukraine and annexing its territory."

Right now, after Ukraine has survived a difficult political crisis, many of us have wound up on different sides of the barricades. The Jews of Ukraine, as all ethnic groups, are not absolutely unified in their opinion towards what is happening in the country. But we live in a democratic country and can afford a difference of opinion. They have tried to scare us (and are continuing their attempts) with "Bandera followers" and "Fascists" attempting to wrest away the helm of Ukrainian society, with imminent Jewish pogroms. Yes, we are well aware that the political opposition and the forces of social protests who have secured changes for the better are made up of different groups. They include nationalistic groups, but even the most marginal do not dare show anti-Semitism or other xenophobic behavior.

On the other hand, Ukrainian Jews hardly felt safe.

"Unfortunately," the letter continued, "we must admit that in recent days stability in our country has been threatened. And this threat is coming from the Russian government, namely—from you personally."

Putin did not take the request to heart. He compared Crimea for Russians to the Temple Mount for Jews and Muslims ("an opinion that should offend Russians, Jews and Muslims alike," commented the Russian American novelist Gary Shetyngart). The interim government assembled in Kiev a few days earlier was in no position to defend the territory. The police were divided and confused. One of those who did resist was the commander of the Ukrainian naval ship *Ternopil*. When the ship's crew heard the call to surrender, the commander of the Ukrainian ship responded, "Russians do not surrender."

"What do you mean Russians?" asked the Russian commander.

"Although my name is Yemielianchenko, I'm Russian by origin. Once in my life I took an oath and I won't break it," the Ukrainian commander answered.

"That is an officer, take an example from him," the Russian commander said to his own men.

That week Slava Vakarchuk went to Donetsk to talk to students. From Donetsk he traveled to Crimea. He wanted to meet with students there, too; he wanted to tell them about the Maidan in Kiev and to learn how they perceived what was happening in Ukraine. Slava had come from Lviv, yet he lived in Kiev and had spent much time in eastern Ukraine, in Belarus, in Russia. He sang in Ukrainian, but spoke Russian easily and willingly. He had millions of fans throughout the former Soviet Union. Sometimes Okean Elzy spent months at a time on tour in Russia; the band played dozens of concerts there during the 2010 tour alone.

Now Slava could not stop thinking about those who had been killed on the Maidan, about their families and their children—and about those who had done the killing, and what they dreamt of at night. He did not want to be a politician; he felt, though, the moral weight of being a role model, especially to young people.

"When you're aware that millions of people listen to you," he said, "you have a responsibility."

Moreover, Slava had an idea, a vision of what Ukraine could and should be: a country guided by civic patriotism. This would be not just a cosmopolitan state—which Slava believed was most likely a quixotic utopia—it would be a truly national state, but a national state of a nation based not on common language or ancestry, but rather on people who made a decision to see their future together. A nation based on civic patriotism would not be "just Babylon"; it would be a democratic society composed of people who had made common choices about what they wanted and what they valued.

When Slava landed at the Simferopol airport on 7 March, he was met by self-described Crimean militiamen. They did not allow him leave the airport; he had come from Ukraine, as a Ukrainian, and Ukraine—they told him—no longer controlled Crimea. The militiamen greeted him with machine guns—although Slava did not believe they meant to hurt him.

"They were very polite, many of them were my fans, they wanted photos for their wives and everything. They kept saying 'sorry,' but there were the guns . . ."

"I did not feel very good that day," Slava told me.

Grandma at War

Lena and Leonid Finberg's daughter, a physician, lived in Moscow with her husband, who was a rabbi, and their children.

"And my granddaughter says to me," Lena told me, "'Grandma, I can't reach you on the phone. Are you still at war?' It even sounds funny: 'Grandma at war.'"

Many times when giving lectures Leonid had spoken about how his was the first generation not to have known war. That had been true for sixty-five years of his life—and then suddenly there was war.

"Tell the story about Putin and Pushkin," said Leonid to Lena. It was a story about their grandchildren.

"The two little ones—five and seven years old—are talking," Lena began. "And the younger one asks the older one: 'What do you think, is President Pushkin a good person?' And the older one answers: 'Pushkin is a poet, like Brodsky, and Putin is the president, but he's bad, he's fighting against Grandma and Grandpa.'"

Nothing Is True
(The Surrealism of Ostriches)

At an equestrian club outside of Moscow, Viktor Yanukovych, now in Russian exile, gave an interview to the BBC. The journalist asked him about the extravagant wealth of Mezhyhirya, the private zoo, the ostriches.

Yanukovych defended himself: "And what's wrong with the fact that I took care of those ostriches? They were just living there—should I have gone around with my eyes closed and pretended not to notice them?"

After all, he liked animals.

In a staged documentary titled *Crimea: The Way Back Home*, Putin starred as the heroic rescuer of Yanukovych, whisking him to safety across the border in the dead of night. A fraudulent referendum and the annexation of Crimea became the occasion for Putin's majestic speech on 18 March 2014:

Dear friends, we have gathered here today in connection with an issue that is of vital, historic significance to all of us. A referendum was held in Crimea on March 16 in full compliance with democratic procedures and international norms. More than 82 percent of the electorate took part in the vote. Over 96 percent of them spoke out in favor of reuniting with Russia. These numbers speak for themselves. . . . In people's hearts and minds, Crimea has always been an inseparable part of Russia. This firm conviction is based on truth and justice and was passed from generation to generation.

The Russia Today camera turned from Putin to faces in the audience: approving, beaming, eyes welling with tears of joy. Hannah Arendt once described old-fashioned lies as a tear in the fabric of reality; the careful observer could perceive the place where the fabric had been torn. Twentieth-century totalitarianism had brought something new: the "modern political lie" involved the creation of a whole other reality. This new reality was seamless; there was no tear to perceive. Vladimir Putin's Crimea speech was seamless.

For Vasyl Cherepanyn, Putin and Yanukovych had created an alternative reality where fascism was anti-fascism, and everything was called what it was not. "Fiction can function as if it were truth," warned the Polish film director Agnieszka Holland, another veteran of Solidarity, when she came to Kiev. The Kievan-born British journalist Peter Pomarantsev titled his book about Putin's Russia *Nothing Is True and Everything Is Possible*.

"When I hear 'nothing is true and everything is possible,'" said Jurko, "I think that violence is very possible."

In Vienna one afternoon in March 2014, I asked Mykola Riabchuk if there had been any news from the Donbas.

"No news is good news," he answered.

Then came news. Local separatists took power in Donetsk and Luhansk; some declared themselves for annexation to Russia, others for local independence of a particular city or autonomy for the Donbas region or "*Novorossiia.*" Literally "New Russia," *Novorossiia* had been a nearly forgotten tsarist term for a region of the Russian empire north of the Black Sea. In April 2014, Putin summoned "*Novorossiia*" back to life, now as a name for a region with undefined borders, potentially including Dnipropetrovsk, Kharkiv, Kherson, Mykolaiv, and Odessa as well as the Donbas. The local separatists were supported by Russian "tourists" and more "little green men."

In April Vyacheslav Ponomarev led an attack on the mayor's office in Slovyansk. Ponomarev, a man in his late forties, was fond of wearing hoodies and baseball caps. Two fingers were missing from his left hand. His men took the elected mayor, a woman, captive; and Ponomarev declared himself mayor of Slovyansk.

On 2 May pro-Russian and pro-Ukrainian demonstrators fought one another with guns, bricks, baseball bats, and Molotov cocktails in the Black Sea port city of Odessa; some half-dozen died in the streets. The fighting reached its climax in front of the Soviet-era Trade Union House, where a fire broke out, killing more than forty pro-Russian demonstrators trapped inside the building.

One week later came Victory Day, the long-celebrated holiday commemorating the Soviet triumph over the Nazis in the Second World War. This year on 9 May a group of armed men calling themselves the Home Guard of the Donetsk People's Republic carried out a raid on the Museum of the Great Patriotic War in Donetsk. They told the staff that they would make use of the exhibited World War II–era weapons to fight the fascists, just as their Soviet predecessors had made use of them to fight the fascists seventy years earlier. "Devoid of any vision of the future," Oleksiy Radynski wrote, "this confrontation was focused on the battles of the past that were to be restarted today, as if for over seven decades they were simply on pause and could now be launched again by pressing the 'play' button on the YouTube channel of Russia Today."

The "play" button could be pressed on several channels at once; what might in the past have been cacophony was now the familiar habit of keeping open multiple windows on a single screen. Some Russian and local volunteers fighting on the side of the separatists declared themselves for Stalin, against Hitler. Others declared themselves for the Russian Orthodox Church, or the legacy of the great tsarist empire, or both, or all three. The *russkii mir*, the "Russian world," a cocktail of nostalgias, stirred together imperial monarchists and ethnic nationalists and international communists, saints and tsars and Bolshevik leaders.

The surreal became the everyday. On the Ukrainian side, former *Berkutovtsy* were fighting next to former members of the Maidan's *Samooborona*. This all happened very quickly. The work of mourning for the Heavenly Hundred had been interrupted. The grieving remained incomplete, the mystery of the Maidan unprocessed. The Ukrainian state was not ready to fight a Russian-sponsored war—which Putin denied he was fighting. The Ukrainian army was being crowd-sourced on the internet.

"When the war began," Serhiy Zhadan told me, "it turned out that we didn't have an army, we didn't have police, we didn't have border guards, we didn't have anything."

The momentum of self-organization continued; civil society proved much more competent than the government. A new Dnipropetrovsk NGO, the National Defense Foundation, coordinated hostage exchanges between the separatists and Ukrainian forces fighting in the Donbas. Members of both Svoboda and Pravyi Sektor played a large role in forming volunteer battalions not entirely under the command of the Ukrainian army. Vasyl believed that the far Right might have faded away from Ukrainian political life had it not been for the war in the east. In this way, too, Svoboda and Pravyi Sektor served the Kremlin's interests: the presence of the far Right justified Putin's purported mission of rescuing persecuted Russian-speakers from the fascists who—Putin claimed—had taken power in Kiev.

Kateryna Iakovlenko, a graduate student in media studies, was one of the curators of Izolyatsia, a contemporary art and discussion center in Donetsk whose space was seized by militants of the Donetsk People's Republic. Kateryna described the separatists as terrorists who transformed Izolyatsia's art space into a prison for those whom they took captive. They arrested the parents of one of Izolyatsia's employees, apparently for their connection to Western decadent art. We were walking from Izolyatsia's space-in-exile in a desolate part of Kiev towards Kontraktova Square, near Mohyla Academy.

"It's very difficult to talk to them on an *intellectual* level," Kateryna said of the separatists who had turned her gallery into a dungeon.

The mix of actors was eclectic; and it was not easy to absorb what was happening quickly enough to respond. In May Moscow dispatched to Donetsk the Vostok Battalion, Chechnya-based Russian special forces. Kateryna recalled that at the time no one in Donetsk seemed to know why the Chechens were there, "they just appeared on the streets like the little green men in Crimea." Many of the Chechens, she noticed, did not speak Russian very well and did not understand why Ukrainian hryvnia came out of the bank machines instead of Russian rubles. She described one occasion when the Chechens fighting on the separatist side organized a meeting on Lenin Square. An elderly local woman appeared and gave one of the Chechens an Orthodox christening to aid his battle against Ukrainian Nazis. For Kateryna everything was surreal in this scene: an Orthodox Christian woman on a communist square christening a Muslim mercenary to kill Ukrainian Nazis who did not exist.

Putin's Sirens

By spring 2014, Crimea was a fait accompli. On 25 May 2014, the same day as the European parliamentary elections, Ukraine held an election "between the Chocolate King and the Gas Princess." The Chocolate King, Petro Poroshenko, won. The far Right got very little support: Oleh Tyahnybok, leader of Svoboda, and Dmytro Yarosh, leader of Pravyi Sektor, won just over and just under 1 percent of the vote, respectively—each receiving fewer votes than Vadim Rabinovich, leader of the Ukrainian Jewish Congress. In the October 2014 parliamentary elections, neither Svoboda nor Pravyi Sektor reached the 5 percent threshold needed to enter parliament. This was in contrast to the far-Right *Freiheitliche Partei Österreichs*, which won close to 20 percent of the Austrian vote in the European parliamentary elections, and Marine Le Pen's far-Right *Front National* in France, which won close to 25 percent. It was as if Freud's ghost were haunting Europe, and Austria and France were gazing at Ukraine through the lens of projection, attributing to others what they could not accept in themselves.

Europeans preferred to put Crimea out of their minds. No one in Brussels wanted to go to war against Russia. The passive condoning of Putin's annexation of the Black Sea peninsula was reminiscent of Neville Chamberlain's "appeasement at Munich," Western Europe's acquiescence to Hitler's annexation of the Sudetenland. Everyone began asking the same question: "What will Putin do? What are Putin's plans? What is Putin thinking?" It was as if there were an unspoken understanding that, once again, the fate of Europe lay in one man's mind.

"He's living in a different world," German chancellor Angela Merkel said after she had spoken by phone to Putin at the very beginning of March. Unlike her predecessor as chancellor, Gerhard Schröder, who traveled to Saint Petersburg in April 2014 to celebrate his seventieth birthday with Putin, Merkel was not enchanted with the Russian dictator. She was sober, and cautious. Merkel was a crisis manager, not a Putin sympathizer—in contrast to many of her fellow Germans, including those on both the far Right and the far Left. Putin's defenders and apologists became known as *"Putin-Versteher"*: those who "understood" Putin. Many of Ukraine's leading writers and intellectuals were Germanists by education; they translated German literature, they lectured in Germany, Austria, and Switzerland. This made the *"Putin-Versteher"* phenomenon all the more painful to them. Some explained Europeans' Russian sympathies by crude financial interests: Russian oligarchs tended to keep their money in Europe; Austrian banks were especially desirable. Gerhard Schröder was chairman of the shareholders' committee of Putin-controlled Gazprom, the largest natural gas company in the world. In 2004, Schröder and his fourth wife adopted a three-year-old girl from a Russian orphanage. The legality of the adoption was murky: the child appeared to be a diplomatic gift—that is, a human bribe. Others explained Putin's attraction as that of a homoerotic *Männerfreundschaft*, a masculinizing ideal of men bonding while drinking vodka in forest lodges and hunting wild boar bare-chested on horseback. Still others explained this by German feelings of guilt towards Russia. The Wehrmacht, SS, and Gestapo had killed millions of Soviet citizens of all nationalities, yet historical memory tended to identify "Soviet" as "Russian." Germans tended to forget less the far more numerous Ukrainians killed during the German occupation and remember more the far fewer Ukrainians who collaborated with it.

His own postwar generation, said a German historian of the Soviet Union named Karl Schlögel, was used to peace and unprepared for Putin. Now it was their task to say aloud that "war is war, annexation is annexation, a lie is a lie." In May 2014 Karl Schlögel came to Kiev and articulated a self-criticism: Germans had long tended to speak "over the heads" of East Europeans. "One spoke rarely *with* Ukrainians, one spoke rather much more *about* them," he wrote. He himself had always looked at Kiev through Moscow. It was only the Maidan that had made him open his eyes, and see that Ukraine was not merely a province of Russia.

My Russian colleagues grew reluctant to talk. One told me only that his friends listened to Russian television, that they thought Putin was right. "I think that social stability is more important than metaphysical freedom," said another, a young woman scholar of religion from the Urals. She might have been paraphrasing Dostoevsky's Grand Inquisitor, who explained to Jesus, when he returned to earth during the Inquisition, why his presence was displeasing: "In the end they will lay their freedom at our feet and say to us: 'Better that you enslave us, but feed us.'" Freedom—insisted the Grand Inquisitor—was a burden too heavy for man; in truth it was not desired.

Putin's approval ratings had hovered around 80 percent since the annexation of Crimea. Even those skeptical of the 80 percent figure admitted that the number must be close to 70 percent in any case. My Russian friend Polina was among this 70 or 80 percent. I had known her for fifteen years. Once she came with me to the writers' village of Peredelkino, where we walked through the mud to visit the Russian literary theorist Viktor Shklovskii's aging daughter. Polina was a gentle, kind, believing Christian. A translator of novels, she had never had any money and never complained. Most of her life she had spent in Moscow, helping to raise her sister's son. In middle age she had married for the first time; she and her husband moved to a village in the countryside. Now Polina felt grateful to Putin. As a Christian, she was grateful to him for supporting "family values," for protecting children from "gay propaganda." Moreover, under his leadership, she experienced how life for ordinary Russians had become much more stable, much more compassionate. He had pulled Russia out of an abyss—Russia, who had always been a "thorn in the flesh of the West," who could trust only herself. She was certain that the West did not need Ukraine and had interfered only to isolate Russia. As for Crimea—Polina wrote—it had been Russian for more than two hundred years.

> The Kosovo Albanians wanted to separate from Serbia—they separated. Take note: non-Serbians separated from Serbians. Crimean Russians wanted to separate from Ukraine—they separated. Take note: Russians (Russians are the overwhelming majority living there) separated from Ukrainians, and then asked to join their own country, Russia. In the first case, it's good and proper, because it plays into the hands of the West, in the second case it's bad and improper because it's good for Russia. Here we see the whole politics of double standards. I know personally several people who live in Crimea, I know people with relatives in Crimea—and from personal conversations and comments, I know that they're all happy to have returned to Russia, they even speak about it this way: "We've returned home." Well, and afterwards the rebellion broke

out in Lugansk and Donetsk oblasts, populated primarily by Russian-speaking citizens who for more than twenty years have been called people of another sort, cattle, and now bandits and criminals as well. After Odessa, frightened that genocide awaits them, they asked for self-government (take note: not separation from Ukraine and annexation to Russia, no, merely self-government and second state language-status for Russian), they were refused, they resolved to win self-government by force. Well, obviously it must be the hand of Moscow, they could not possibly be allowed to separate. And now let's recall Chechnya . . . the West treated Russia with such contempt for her actions in Chechnya and for not wanting to give Chechnya independence! And what of the fact that the West is not now advising Ukraine to let go of those two oblasts? Here again—double standards. . . . Because of Crimea, and afterwards what was happening in *Novorossiia*, the West began to impose sanctions, and in response Russia imposed her own. Of course, the economic situation in Russia has become complicated, but name a period in history when the West in some way or another has not imposed sanctions against Russia (the Soviet Union)? We have always lived amidst the ill will of the West, so this is hardly anything new. Yes, prices have risen, yes there is inflation, but the lack of European products in shops is barely noticeable. The stores are not empty, the shelves are bursting, and that it's not possible to buy Spanish ham or Parmesan cheese is no great loss—these things don't find their way into the daily shopping basket of the average customer anyway . . . In short, if the Western mass media claim that due to the restriction of European products in Russia, people are dying of hunger, don't believe it. It's a lie. The main thing, perhaps, is this: the tendency of the West to preach to us from a position of power, to inflict suffering by means of sanctions, only evokes distinct

disenchantment, resentment, and a natural disinclination to yield
to the threat. And yes: pride in our president, who has proven to
be an excellent politician and who consistently vindicates Russia's
interests . . .

Returning to Ukraine, I understand that Ukraine is—to put
it delicately—feeling hurt because of Crimea and *Novorossiia*.
But Ukraine herself is to blame, she made a mess of the peninsula, and lo and behold people have had enough of suffering.
She made a mess of the Russian-speaking regions, and they've
had enough. And the military actions themselves! Have you
read about or seen somewhere in the Western mass media how
the Ukrainian army has shelled schools, hospitals, residential
neighborhoods, kindergartens? Have you seen the dead children? Do they write about that in the West? I've already asked
about Odessa. And about the fact that people are fleeing from
Ukraine to Russia, tens of thousands of refugees—do they write
about that? That Ukraine, our neighbor, as a result of careful
work by the West (over the course of twenty-three years) has
become Russia's enemy—how are we supposed to like that?
And now in power there we have, if not fascists, then the kind
of nationalists who are no better than fascists and at the head of
state an oligarch, and what's good about that? Russia supported
the previous government, not these bandits. And again Russia is
to blame?

Polina concluded her letter with this thought: "It is a pity
that Ukraine is no longer our friend, thanks to the West. Poor
Ukraine has turned out to be a bargaining chip in Western
games against Russia—likely that is all that can be said by way
of an epitaph. What happens further, Marci, will be as God wills.
Time will tell."

The sad irony was that my Ukrainian colleagues felt abandoned by the West. Katia Mishchenko was a translator of German literature. She and her husband Vasyl both had strong ties to Germany, and they were hurt by what Vasyl described as "Western blindness" about the Maidan. "The context is somehow beyond the Western imagination," Vasyl said. "Yes, the far Right was there, but it was a real revolution, and in a real revolution all the oppositional forces are present." Vasyl had anticipated international protests in support of the Maidan, "but there was nothing, there was no real international solidarity."

Jurko Prochasko suspected that the West's failure to understand what was happening in Ukraine betrayed a lack of desire to understand: events in Ukraine had laid bare what had long been repressed in Western consciousness. He believed that, not only Russians, but also Europeans had proven easily seduced by Putin's sirens, the bewitching female creatures of Greek myths whose songs proved irresistible to all who heard them. Odysseus, when passing the sirens at sea, ordered his soldiers to block their own ears with beeswax, and to tie Odysseus to the mast. Orpheus protected himself in a different way: he overcame the voices of the sirens with the still more alluring music of his own lyre. Jurko preferred Orpheus's choice.

During a 2015 lecture in Kiev, the anthropologist Shalini Randeria spoke about the Indian independence movement leader Mahatma Gandhi, who when once asked about Western civilization had replied, "It would be a very good idea." This

"would-be very good idea" was the "Europe" desired so passionately on the Maidan: "Europe" meant the opposite of *proizvol*—
it meant human rights, the rule of law, the dignity of being
treated as a subject, not an object. This idea of Europe was, as
a philosophical distinction went, perhaps more *eidos* than fact,
more essence than the particular, imperfect instantiation. In Edmund Husserl's phenomenology, when we perceived an apple,
we grasped not only the particular apple in front of us, but also
the universal essence of "appleness" and "redness." Our intui-
tion extracted the ideal essence from the empirical object. Vasyl
believed that Ukrainians were filling the signifier "Europe" with
its ideal content.

For Husserl this ideal content of Europe was quite specific:
Europe was "the historical teleology of the infinite goals of reason." When the Nazi regime cast Husserl out of the university
for his Jewish origins, he was in despair: Europe had deviated
from its true path, irrationalism had led to barbarism. He came
to Prague to deliver the lectures he could no longer deliver in
Germany. There in the Czechoslovak capital, in November
1935, Husserl spoke about the Enlightenment's spirit of learn-
ing, its optimistic search for truth.

"We possess an undying testimony to this spirit in the glori-
ous 'Ode to Joy' of Schiller and Beethoven. It is only with painful feelings," Husserl lamented, "that we can understand this
hymn today."

In 1972, the European Union adopted the "Ode to Joy" of

Beethoven's Ninth Symphony as its anthem. At 10:30 am on Saturday morning, 22 March 2014, musicians from the Odessa Philharmonic and Opera Chorus walked into Odessa's *privoz*, a crowded indoor market where people were scaling whitefish and cleaning mackerel gills and weighing bags of anchovies. There among the market stalls filled with scents of sardines and smoked herring they played "Ode to Joy"—drowning, for a moment, the voices of Putin's sirens.

Zhidobandera *on the Dnipro*

In late June 2015, my historian colleague Igor Shchupak's brother-in-law picked me up at the airport in Dnipropetrovsk. On the rear windshield of his cherry-red car was a sticker: a white triangle outlined in matching cherry red. Against the white background was an image of a woman's shoe with a stiletto heel, vaguely suggestive of Cinderella's glass slipper, albeit in black.

I asked Igor's brother-in-law about the sticker. The car belonged to his sister, he told me. He explained that driving in Ukraine tended to be somewhat wild: fast, competitive, lawless. Women put these stickers on their cars to alert the male drivers to their presence. He always drove more carefully when he saw a car with the sticker; it was the only considerate thing for a man to do.

Dnipropetrovsk, a postindustrial commercial center, was a very post-Soviet city. The streets were wide; their names had not been changed since the fall of the Soviet Union: Karl Marx Avenue remained, as did Komsomol Street, Kirov Avenue, and Lenin Embankment.

"What are you doing there?" a friend from Moscow asked anxiously in a text message. "Is it dangerous?"

No, I assured her, it was not dangerous in Dnipropetrovsk. In any case, not today.

Dnipropetrovsk was gray and wet—but not frightening. There were fountains and little buses Ukrainians call *marshrutkas* and a carousel lit in the evening with warm golden lights. Next to the carousel, a five-story shopping mall named "Europe," with floor-to-ceiling windows, housed the Gap, Marks and Spencer, and a sushi restaurant. Two dozen or so yards away, on Karl Marx Avenue, stood a giant sculpture named "Slipper": a stiletto-heeled shoe made of 156 stainless steel pots and 324 stainless steel lids extending two floors above the ground. It glittered strangely.

A twenty-minute walk away from the shopping mall and the carousel and the stiletto slipper was a less glittering installation: photographs of the Heavenly Hundred surrounded by flowers and decorated in yellow and blue with the slogan *"Heroes do not die."* Elsewhere in the city huge billboards declared Ukrainian patriotism in the Russian language: *We take pride in living in Dnipropetrovsk! We are Ukrainian!*

Russian-speaking Dnipropetrovsk, on the Dnipro River deep

in southeastern Ukraine, some 120 miles distant from the war in the Donbas, had become a bastion of Ukrainian patriotism. A week after Yanukovych had fled Ukraine, acting Ukrainian president Oleksandr Turchynov had appointed the oligarch Ihor Kolomoyskyi governor of Dnipropetrovsk Oblast. Kolomoyskyi held Cypriot and Israeli as well as Ukrainian citizenship; he was a proud Jew and a Ukrainian patriot. He was also a middle-aged man drawn into a masculinity contest with Vladimir Putin. At stake was the fate of a country. Shortly after his appointment as governor, Kolomoyskyi appeared in a t-shirt with *"Zhidobandera"* written in red against a black background, the colors of the Ukrainian Insurgent Army, and a symbol fusing the Jewish menorah with a trident, the Ukrainian state's coat of arms. He privately funded military and security battalions to ensure that Russian-allied separatists did not take power in Dnipropetrovsk. He also offered a reward for captured "little green men."

A five-minute walk from the stiletto slipper on Karl Marx Avenue stood a 50,000-square-meter complex of interlocking buildings forming the shape of a menorah, best visible from the sky. The Menorah complex was a surreal juxtaposition of a Donald Trump–style luxury hotel with marble floors and high ceilings, and a high-security military industrial compound with gray metal doors lining windowless corridors. Sedona red marble floors reflected the images of those who stepped on them. Sand-colored walls suggested Jerusalem stone; on these walls a sculptor had re-created the facades of prominent buildings in

Ekaterinoslav, Dnipropetrovsk's tsarist-era incarnation. There was a kosher restaurant, a coffee shop, a ballroom, a concert hall, conference rooms, an art gallery, and a Museum of Jewish Memory and Holocaust in Ukraine. The museum concluded with a room devoted to other historical instances of ethnic cleansing and genocide. There was no sign explaining the artifacts related to the Ukrainian-Polish ethnic cleansing of the 1940s; the student who guided me through the museum explained that curators had been unable to decide what to say.

In a separate hall close to the ethnic cleansing exhibit was another display: Kolomoyskyi's personal collection of heirloom timepieces—Renaissance and neoclassical, adorned with Greek deities, ornate cherubs, and reclining seductresses strumming on lyres. Hundreds of antique table clocks in bronze and marble and gold.

Smart Kids Like You

After he had shown me the golden clocks, my student guide led me through corridors to a classroom. There two professors of history, women in early middle age, were leading a seminar for fourteen- and fifteen-year-old aspiring historians. All had strong feelings about the revolution that had just taken place in Kiev.

"I was against it," said one girl.

"And I was against it," added a boy named Stanislav.

Their teachers were displeased.

"You were against the Revolution of Dignity?" asked one professor.

"I—let's say—it's not that I was against it, but I think they didn't do it the right way. I mean the methods they used," said Stanislav.

He had spent a lot of time in Kiev during the Maidan,

Stanislav explained. His father had been serving in the military in the capital.

"Stanislav," his teacher said, "do you remember how it began? Stanislav, we do remember how it began, don't we? On 30 November there was an attack on peaceful students, who were absolutely not threatening anyone. Stanislav, you're leading this discussion, so to speak, you started it. So please tell us, do you remember—this happened on 30 November, and how did ordinary residents of Kiev react?"

"It's clear enough, there was a big uproar."

"And then the government's reaction?"

"There was one reaction—they thought it was right."

"They agreed with the many thousands of demonstrators, spreading themselves throughout Kiev, did they?"

"No. They understood that they were acting improperly."

"And afterwards, when residents of Ukraine, and not only of Kiev, started to trek to Kiev? When women stood up and said, 'I imagined that my son, my daughter could have been there,' when people were hiding in Saint Michael's cathedral—we do remember that, yes?"

Several of the students tried to speak at once.

"Berkut," one girl protested, "—they're also people, they were just forced. I have relatives who work in the militia, in Berkut—look, they're just simple people, just like we are, this is just their job. This is how it is these days with jobs. They told them—no,

I'm just explaining how the leadership talks—they told them, 'Either you do what we say, or you're fired.'"

"It's terrible," interrupted another girl. "I mean terrible what the government did . . . I'm not saying that the revolutionaries were all saints. There were some who from behind the barricades threw bricks at Berkut's heads. But you also can't say that Berkut was saintly."

"*Kids*," their teacher cut them off, "international observers are talking about the fact that a civil society is forming, a civil society that—let us suppose—did not exist a year ago. It simply did not exist. Truly a conscious society of citizens of Ukraine who understand that this is their homeland. This is very important. Yes, there are very many 'but's.' Nevertheless it remains the fact: a conscious society. And *smart kids like you, you* are building that society. The main thing now is to have your own position, and that position should be the correct one. Ukraine is our homeland. We should do everything so that we, our children, and our grandchildren live well here. And move forward."

Now the second professor spoke as well. "We have never discussed the twentieth century the way we're discussing it now. I don't like to talk about the history of the twentieth century. Because I am a woman. And the twentieth century in Ukraine was death and killing. And I, as a woman, have not wanted to talk about that. Until this year. This year we should talk about the history of the twentieth century, because we should understand what is happening now."

After all—she reminded her students—so many of her colleagues were out there on the Maidan. And the young historian from the Ukrainian Catholic University, Bohdan Solchanyk, was killed there.

"We understood perfectly . . ."

Igor Shchupak, director of the Ukrainian Institute for Holocaust Studies, whose brother-in-law had picked me up at the airport, now took me to meet his friend, Pavlo Khazan. In the parking lot, Igor showed me Pavlo's van: it was a dark-brownish-gray color and pierced with bullet holes.

Inside a tall building Pavlo was waiting for us. He looked healthy and fit and no older than forty; he was bald with a very warm smile and kind eyes still not completely healed from a tear gas attack that winter. Pavlo did not look like a man who drove a van with bullet holes.

I asked Pavlo about his life before the Maidan.

"Normal life, you mean? That seems like a very long time ago."

A native of Dnipropetrovsk, Pavlo was a physicist who worked on clean energy; his pre-Maidan activism had centered around the organization Friends of the Earth of Ukraine. He had been a delegate to the European Green Party; his political engagement and his scientific research were of a piece.

"Everything that I have done for the last twenty years of my conscious adult life is civic activity, ecological activity, political-ecological activity," Pavlo said, "and the whole point of what I've been doing is, of course, to build democracy in our society."

Pavlo spoke as if he had emerged from Denis Diderot's circle of Encyclopedists in eighteenth century France: he was the model Enlightenment figure, for whom the pursuit of pure science and the building of democracy belonged to a whole. He believed passionately in nonviolent civic engagement, in the guiding power of autonomous reason, and in the potential of scientific knowledge to advance human freedom. He spoke Russian with the expressiveness of someone who was practiced at presenting his research to different audiences and articulating his ideas to others. He was self-confident, but also self-aware about the boundaries of knowledge, and not hesitant to admit when he was uncertain.

Before the Maidan, Pavlo had been publicly critical of Yanukovych's government; and he had been advised to leave the country. There had been opportunities: Pavlo spoke very good English and was well connected in Brussels. He did not want to emigrate, though; he wanted to build democracy in Ukraine.

As we talked, it was ever more difficult to imagine Pavlo driving a van pierced with bullet holes. It was much easier to imagine him as a learned, compassionate uncle playing chess with his nieces and nephews, or reading Tolstoy to them.

The beginning of the Maidan was the end of normal life.

"That was it," Pavlo said, "we understood perfectly where this was all going."

My prekrasno ponimali. We understood perfectly. Pavlo was not the only one who used this expression time and again in relation to the Maidan. Iryna Iaremko, too, had described her thinking as she organized the buses going from Lviv to Kiev: "*We understood perfectly that we were not going back, only forward.*" "*We understood perfectly*" was an affirmation of lucidity, the feeling that as of a certain moment, everything was absolutely clear.

In November 2013, Pavlo and a small group in Dnipropetrovsk —Friends of the Earth members, activists from youth organizations, a few ordinary local lunatics, as Pavlo described them— began Dnipropetrovsk's own Maidan on European Square, the site of the shopping center and the carousel and the stainless steel stiletto slipper. Some were radical, some liberal; most were peaceful, a few eagerly anticipated violence. Pavlo was committed to nonviolence; he rejected the Leninist dictum that ends justified means. Democracy, he believed, could not be built using undemocratic methods.

Often Pavlo traveled to the Maidan in Kiev. In the meantime, in Dnipropetrovsk the modest group of activists gathered every day on European Square. Then came the laws of mid-January and the understanding that the country was headed towards dictatorship; and this brought more people to European Square, people from very different milieux, people who otherwise would never have met one another. On 26 January Pavlo and other activists went to the regional administration building to ask the regional government to take the side of the people against the dictatorship laws. It was cold; on the streets there was ice and snow. When they arrived at the administration building, they were met by *titushki* with baseball bats and spade shafts. There were uniformed militiamen in full gear as well, nearly as many militiamen as there were demonstrators.

Pavlo and two other activists were chosen as delegates to negotiate with the authorities. They approached the militia, asking the men to put down their clubs and shields. For a moment it seemed to Pavlo they had been persuasive. Then he realized that the militia was protecting the *titushki*, that this was a setup.

"Were you afraid?" I asked him.

"Well, of course it was *unpleasant*," answered Pavlo.

No one knew what would come next, whether the demonstrators would be beaten or shot or killed. There were many women among them, there were children and grandparents. Pavlo felt a responsibility to protect, at the very least, those who were most vulnerable. He understood, too, that once the *titushki* used violence, the demonstrators would feel compelled to respond with violence, and this would become a pretext for mass arrests and shootings. Afterwards no one would know who had been shooting or from where. And so Pavlo opposed any violence at all, "because we understood perfectly that it was a provocation."

The purpose of the demonstration was to persuade the regional authorities to protect the democratic interests of their constituency. Pavlo was determined to talk to them and ensure that there would be no cruelty towards citizens. Things did not go that way. One of the other two delegates was abruptly arrested. Pavlo had just been with him; they had been trying to keep the demonstrators physically separated from the *titushki*, his fellow delegate had been shielding a woman with his own body. Then came the tear gas, and suddenly Pavlo was blinded. A friend took him away; later Pavlo headed to the militia headquarters; when he arrived, he saw a large number of handcuffed people in unmarked cars. Throughout the city people were being arrested, including people who had not taken part in the demonstration at all, who seemed to have been chosen at random.

Friends advised Pavlo to leave Ukraine as quickly as possible, and to avoid the Dnipropetrovsk airport, where the police were waiting for him. And so he traveled by car from Dnipropetrovsk to Kiev, and by plane from Kiev to Brussels. Pavlo believed he had been allowed to board the plane to Brussels only because police communications between Dnipropetrovsk and Kiev were so poor.

Pavlo stayed first in Belgium, then in the Netherlands, until Yanukovych had fled Ukraine. When in early March Pavlo returned to Dnipropetrovsk, he discovered that there was, in effect, no government operating in the city at all.

When Ihor Kolomoyskyi was chosen as governor, Pavlo felt gratified—in part because Kolomoyskyi represented the Jewish community. He was not an uncontroversial choice for governor: after all, he was an oligarch. On the other hand, "we all understood perfectly that some changes were necessary." And Kolomoyskyi was the kind of person who could make changes happen quickly. Pavlo had not known Kolomoyskyi personally, but now he welcomed him on behalf of local activists. In turn, Kolomoyskyi invited Pavlo to become one of his advisors.

There had been no time after the Maidan to enjoy the prospect of the rule of law; almost within days, the revolution had turned into war. In April 2014 wounded Ukrainian soldiers were already arriving at the Dnipropetrovsk airport. In May 2014 Pavlo established the National Defense Foundation to defend the state; he and his co-workers collected donations from small businessmen, from ordinary people.

"And so I, an ecologist in peacetime, a person occupied with physics, with ecology, with sustainable development, I became a person occupied with the defense of the state."

Pavlo's first university degree had been in radio physics; as a reserve officer, his training had been in military communications. Now he began setting up encrypted radio communications for the Ukrainian army.

"At this time," Pavlo explained, "our state and the ministry of defense were doing nothing."

Many of the communications specialists Pavlo worked with on those first projects had since been killed, including his friend Iasha. For a long time Pavlo had hoped that Iasha was still alive, perhaps taken hostage . . . but over time the evidence accumulated. Pavlo was not even certain where Iasha had died.

The National Defense Foundation provided first-aid supplies and training in tactical medicine. It also negotiated hostage exchanges. Given that he was among those they would most like to see killed, Pavlo did not negotiate with the separatists himself. For a time he had been traveling to the front about once a week, then he began to be actively hunted; once the separatists tried to kill him. Pavlo preferred not to dwell on that. In any case, it was his colleague Olga who negotiated with the separatists for the release of hostages. Olga was younger than Pavlo, just over thirty.

"It is very complex, very difficult, very dangerous and very delicate work. And she's a frail, small girl."

Negotiations were unpredictable. It could be, Pavlo explained, that today the separatists would call and say they were prepared to exchange hostages. And then Olga and a small group of their colleagues would get in her car and drive to a site on the border between government-controlled Ukraine and the separatist-controlled territories. If she succeeded, she would return to

Dnipropetrovsk with the hostages. Sometimes they managed to negotiate the release of hostages without exchanges. Sometimes they exchanged prisoners. Sometimes they failed entirely. The last two times negotiations had failed; Olga had stayed in the war zone for more than a week and in the end she had brought back no one.

"It's a complex, psychological, multifactor 'game,' let's call it," Pavlo said.

"And it works out sometimes?" I asked.

"It works out more often than not. And we've brought back many more wartime hostages than the government has. Many more."

By now Olga and her team had returned to Dnipropetrovsk with dozens of hostages. Some had been mutilated.

"Does the Ukrainian Army take hostages for the purpose of exchanging them?" I asked Pavlo.

"Yes. That is, sometimes we make use of those hostages in our possession and do an exchange. A hostage for a hostage."

Pavlo was not entirely comfortable with how the Ukrainian side treated its prisoners. As far as he knew, the hostages who were taken by the Ukrainian army officially as prisoners of war were treated humanely. He also knew, though, that the Ukrainian side sometimes took hostages who were not formally declared as such, and that it also happened that the Ukrainian side brutalized its prisoners.

"But that's human psychology," Pavlo told me, "that's war."

Pavlo would have preferred a more elevated human race. In the absence of that, he would have preferred that international organizations intervene to assure humane treatment of prisoners by both sides. Officially, there was no war; the Ukrainian government had declared only an "Anti-Terrorist Operation." Pavlo did not like this: if there was a war, it should be declared a war and international law should be enforced. He was a person who very much liked law.

In the meantime, absent the rule of law, the most important thing was saving lives. Given that, Pavlo and Olga were willing to talk to anyone.

"For us," said Pavlo openly, "it's unimportant with whom we're carrying out negotiations. For us it's unimportant that this is a terrorist organization, because we know that in the Donetsk People's Republic and in the Lugansk People's Republic, there is not one but many terrorist groups. There are groups of gangsters who feud with one another, fight against one another, kill one another. But if we can find a common language with a group of gangsters and bring home a Ukrainian citizen, I consider that a good thing."

"For us, for Jews . . ." Pavlo began.

Judaism, as Pavlo understood his own religion, taught that the highest value was human life. And so he would talk to anyone if it meant saving someone's life. Hanging in Pavlo's office was a *Zhidobandera* banner; it was blue on yellow, the colors of the Ukrainian flag, and fused the trident with the star of David.

Pavlo also showed me his *Zhidobandera* hooded sweatshirt, red on black, like Kolomoyskyi's t-shirt. Pavlo was not very observant, but he had friends who were very religious Jews, and they violated the Sabbath to go to war on behalf of Ukrainian independence. This was more than permissible, it was a *mitzvah*, a Jewish commandment, if human life was at stake.

"We understand perfectly," Pavlo said to me, "that what's important for us is saving people's lives."

Before Igor and I left, Pavlo showed me the upright piano he had played on the Dnipropetrovsk Maidan. It was an old piano, an Ibach that a friend had restored for him. Pavlo told me a joke about East European Jews emigrating to Israel: if a Jew arrived in Israel with a violin, he was a violinist. If he arrived with no violin, he was a pianist. Pavlo was a pianist. Now he sat down at the piano and began to play a tango written by the Polish composer Jerzy Petersburski, "This Is the Last Sunday." Igor sang. Pavlo told me that Jerzy Petersburski had been a friend of his grandfather, Boris, who was a trombone player. In the 1930s, Boris had organized the first jazz band in Dnipropetrovsk. Jazz was forbidden then, it was considered anti-Soviet, and so the band declared itself to be an "ensemble of national instruments," including a mandolin.

"God plays man," added Igor, "and man plays the mandolin."

The Volunteer Movement

The imperial ambitions of Putin, the irresponsibility of Ukrainian politicians, the corruption, the reluctance of the West to get involved—for Ukrainians it was like moving in the darkness, Serhiy Zhadan wrote, not knowing where they were, unable to make out where they were headed.

By the time I met Pavlo Khazan in June 2015 the Donbas had become a site of humanitarian catastrophe. Donetsk, a city of nearly one million people, had been shelled by both sides. Hundreds of thousands of refugees arrived in Kiev, Lviv, and other Ukrainian towns and cities. Lena and Leonid Finberg's son Arseniy, the father of two small children and the owner of a travel agency who was very good with logistics, founded a refugee center in the Podil neighborhood of Kiev. In an interview with a Jewish newspaper, Arensiy explained that Jewish values strengthened something he already felt as a civic obligation: the impossibility of standing aside when the person next to him was suffering.

The refugee center in Podil was housed in a dilapidated building, staffed by volunteers, and sustained by donations from ordinary people. Whole rooms filled up with used clothing. In a room with chunks of paint chipped off the walls Arseniy set up laptops and a printer and mounted a monitor to show which number in the queue was being called. A huge tent created a recreational space with books and toys. Time-wearied stuffed animals greeted those fleeing the war: a green-and-yellow dragon, a white dog with black spots in a red cap, a long-nosed brown mouse wearing a yellow t-shirt. The refugee center was not funded by the government; it was another feat of self-organization.

"That Ukraine exists, that it has not disappeared, is not thanks to the government but in spite of the government," Serhiy Zhadan told me.

There was a paradox in volunteers like Arseniy and Pavlo mobilizing to defend a state, aware that their mobilization was needed precisely because that state did not function. Pavlo spoke soberly about how the goal of his foundation was to make itself obsolete: to set an example for the government about how to be practical, useful, and competent. Many of the soldiers who had died, Pavlo told me, could have been saved by fellow soldiers with basic medical training and kits. Pavlo's foundation organized first-aid courses, schooling military recruits in tactical medicine. The volunteer movement was doing the job of the government: training soldiers, supplying the army, negotiating hostage exchanges, housing and feeding refugees.

This was not only an exercise in living the absurd. The choice that everyone in Kiev had to make during the Maidan was the choice everyone in the east had to make during the "Russian Spring." For his own city of Kharkiv, in northeastern Ukraine close to the Russian border, Serhiy Zhadan called spring 2014 "the moment of truth." The political scientist Tatiana Zhurzhenko described it as "the end of ambivalence." She, too, was from Kharkiv and had experienced the splits across families, across friendships. To be pro-Ukrainian in Kharkiv, Luhansk, or Donetsk, in Dnipropetrovsk or Odessa, was to be pro-European, she said. The war in the east was about where Europe ended and where it began. Tatiana chose Ukraine. She had lost friends.

In Dnipropetrovsk, too, the moment of decision came only after the massacre on the Maidan. Ihor Kolomoyskyi's gangster-like presence and desire to challenge Putin's masculinity with his own made the choice for Ukraine practically possible: the oligarch-turned-governor used his own wealth to arm men at a moment when the Ukrainian army, "barefoot and naked," was not ready to fight. Kolomoyskyi provided weapons, but it was the people of Dnipropetrovsk who put themselves forward and volunteered to use them, emphasized Oleg Marchuk, a broad-shouldered local businessman who traded in microelectronics.

"The volunteer movement that arose in Dnipropetrovsk is unprecedented," he told me.

Oleg cared about good music and cars and food and wine. In late June 2015 he had just returned to Dnipropetrovsk from the Alfa Jazz Fest in Lviv. He had made the fourteen-hour trip over rough roads in his Lexus. Now he drove me to the fashionable Myshi Bliakhera café on Karl Marx Avenue, where waiters and waitresses served meals arranged like modern art. Years ago, Oleg had studied mechanical engineering. Those were days when he had also been a competitive runner: eight hundred meters in two minutes, one kilometer in two minutes forty-four seconds, ten kilometers in thirty-seven minutes. Now he had gained weight and looked more like a bodybuilder than a runner: his arms were burly and his hands were thick—just right for his extravagant wristwatch and oversized platinum wedding band.

Oleg cared about being a businessman; it was who he wanted to be. He enjoyed the competition of the market, just as he had once enjoyed competitive running; in business like in athletics, though, competition was satisfying only when conditions were impartial. Dnipropetrovsk was a city of middle-class businessmen, he explained, and while by rights people like himself should be setting the tone, in fact it was impossible to do business normally amidst all the corruption. Oleg wanted to play the game by fair rules, and he became an activist on behalf of legality, lobbying for the rule of law in the marketplace. In 2008 he founded an organization of business owners and top-level managers who refused to take bribes.

"Is it possible to do business at all without taking part in the system of bribes?" I asked him.

"It's not possible," he answered. "That is, all businessmen to some degree or another pay bribes. Maybe there's someone who says he hasn't paid, but I don't know any such person. I'm being honest. Everything depends on whether you pay more or less, but sooner or later you have to pay."

Oleg clarified: it was understood that of course they all had to *pay* bribes; what distinguished the members of his organization was that they refused to *take* bribes. So the group was highly selective. All of its members supported the Maidan.

Oleg wanted to be a normal, successful businessman—not a worker or a peasant, not an oligarch or a gangster, just a Western-style corporate executive operating in a rule-of-law state. He very much identified with his class and milieu; and he was skeptical about the workers.

"The proletariat here made its revolution in 1917 with Lenin, and now they're tired," he said.

Others were not yet tired, or were not tired any longer. Dnipropetrovsk had changed in the past two years: the "Cossack spirit" had returned. The city had become more confident, more sure of itself. People had asked themselves hard questions about their values, about "what a person is willing to give his life for."

"Everything else is a half-value," Oleg said.

If war did come to Dnipropetrovsk, he was certain that people would fight. The mood at the moment was very patriotic: everyone would defend his own street, his own home.

"I don't know if Putin understands this or not, but if they come here, we will likely slaughter them."

The café was loud and crowded, the tables were close together. Oleg looked at the people around us.

"Every second person sitting here will take up arms."

The Specter of Communism

Iurii Fomenko, a small businessman in Dnipropetrovsk, did take up arms. In spring 2014 he volunteered to evacuate children from unsafe areas. In August he volunteered for the Ukrainian army; the following nine months he spent fighting in the Donbas, in a rural area between Debaltseve and Horlivka. He had experience: he had served in the Soviet army in the 1980s. Iurii was sturdy and clean-shaven, with pointed ears and pale blue eyes.

"The first time I was looking in the submachine gun for the specter of imperialism—and the second time for the specter of communism," Iurii told me.

In provoking separatist rebellions against the Ukrainian state, Iurii believed the Kremlin had miscalculated: precisely those Russian-speaking regions of eastern Ukraine Putin had assumed would start flying Russian flags had produced the most volunteer battalions to fight the separatists.

"Dnipropetrovsk was the center of defense," he told me. "Russia was shocked by this: these very regions, where the Russians thought they would be greeted with bread and salt . . ."

Iurii volunteered not only "to defend his own land, his own state, the territory of his grandfathers," but also to defend "spiritual values," in particular those spiritual values at odds with their Moscow counterparts.

"What does being Ukrainian mean to you?" I asked him.

"The mentality of a Ukrainian is not the *kolkhoz*, it's self-sufficiency, everyone is a unique personality. Russians are more collective: they catch a wild boar, drag it back, a woman divides it up."

These Ukrainian values in any case had nothing to do with ethnicity or language, and Iurii insisted that the language issue was imaginary, a creation of Russian television. In Dnipropetrovsk Russian was the dominant language of most of the population.

"Everything is constructed on absurdities," Iurii said.

In the beginning of his time in the army, Iurii commanded about fifteen men; later he became commander of about one hundred—plus one military cat, named Kozlenok; Iurii showed me Kozlenok's photograph on his smartphone.

Many of Iurii's friends had already died in this war, older people as well, people who told him that the Germans had been less cruel to them during the Second World War than the Russians were now. Iurii himself could not say for certain whether that was objectively true.

"There's fear," he said, "it's a very bad feeling."

"Did you kill any of the separatists?" I asked him.

"It's complicated, let's not answer that. It's complicated."

A Civilizational Choice

"What does 'Ukraine' mean to you?" I asked Valerii and Elena Kozachek, Dnipropetrovsk activists of the same generation as Oleg Marchuk and Iurii Fomenko.

"Oh, we so love Ukraine!" Elena said expressively.

"What kind of Ukraine do you want?"

"Free, European," she answered. "It doesn't matter, let it be European or any kind of progressive. With values—the values accepted all over the world—so that we would have them here, too. So that it would no longer happen that we choose for our president a man with two criminal convictions, who went to prison for stealing hats."

Elena and her husband had both stood on the Maidan in Dnipropetrovsk—not all day, because unlike in Kiev, in Dnipropetrovsk people gathered there only in the evenings. They were there every day, though, through the whole winter—except when it seemed unsafe; during those times Valerii, who like Oleg Marchuk was formidably built, went alone. Their grown son had been in Kiev then, on the Maidan there, trying to conceal from his parents that he stayed even when it was dangerous.

For Valerii and Elena the Maidan meant the end of vassalship to Russia. The end, full stop. They were thinking about the Holodomor, the famine of the 1930s, when Soviet Ukraine suffered a bad harvest, and Stalin's men came and took every last piece of grain, condemning millions to starvation. Valerii's aunt, his mother's older sister, had been only five years old when she had died of hunger. That was in 1933, before Valerii's mother was born. Even after all these years had passed, his family still lived in the shadow of the famine, shaped by those absences, by the older relatives who were not there.

"The cause was Moscow," Valerii said. "The ones who killed them—I don't want to know them, they're our enemies. And they've always been our enemies. In Soviet schools, in the Soviet Union, they lied to us, they told lies. Do you understand? The whole history of Russia, it's all invented. There's not a word of truth there, not a single word of truth."

Russia had stolen even the name—"Rus"—from Ukraine, which had its origins some thousand years ago in the medieval east Slavic federation named Kievan Rus. History mattered to Valerii. He repeated himself because he wanted to be absolutely certain I had understood: "The Soviet Union caused the famine in 1933. The Soviet Union together with Hitler unleashed the war, and ordinary people paid the price for it. This was *my personal motivation* for the fight on the Maidan: the complete break with Russia and the former Soviet Union."

"The Maidan," he said, "was like a period, the end."

Valerii and Elena regretted that they had to speak Russian to me—let it be any language other than the language of their enemy, who lied and stole and murdered. They were reading more and more in Ukrainian these days, trying to improve their Ukrainian. Russian was their stronger language, but unlike Pavlo Khazan and Iurii Fomenko and Oleg Marchuk, who were more self-assured, they were a bit ashamed, as if the Russian language belonged more to Stalin and Putin than to themselves.

"We're a European country, do you understand?" Valerii asked me.

Theirs was "a civilizational choice": to be free of Russia, to be part of Europe, where Ukraine had been three or four centuries ago. "Civilization," a neologism of the eighteenth century French Enlightenment, meant that the disorder and brutality of the state of nature had been overcome. That was what Valerii and Elena wanted, and this was how they understood themselves. It upset them that Europeans now thought of Ukraine as a country at war. The war was taking place in a tiny part of Ukraine; the front was more than a hundred miles away.

"You can come here with your children, it's absolutely no

problem," Valerii assured me. "Nothing will happen. Absolutely nothing will happen."

It was true that there was no war in Dnipropetrovsk. The city did not even feel edgy.

"And you're not at all afraid that the war will come here?" I asked.

"No, no," Valerii said.

"We are afraid," Elena said. It was the only time she contradicted her husband.

"I'm not afraid," Valerii said proudly.

"We are civilized people," Elena said to me as she shook my hand in parting. "We understand you, but you don't understand us."

Black Lizard on Red Square

In the kosher café inside Menorah, Tetiana Portnova, the younger sister of my historian colleague, Andriy Portnov, introduced me to her friends Ihor Petrovsky and Victoria Narizhna. Ihor was a stylistic contrast to stocky businessmen like Oleg Marchuk, Iurii Fomenko, and Valerii Kozachek: at forty-two, Ihor was thin and artsy, with a skater's dyed blond hair, and a moustache and a goatee and razor stubble framing a chiseled nose. His fingers were slender, his manicured nails painted in clear gloss. He wore a small diamond earring in his left ear. His wife, Victoria, wore silver earrings that dangled, a sleeveless turtleneck the color of red wine, and large tortoiseshell glasses. Waves of thick hair were dyed a burnt orange. Victoria was as much unlike Elena as Ihor was unlike Valerii. Yet they were all on the same side.

The Maidan was Ihor's third revolution—and Victoria's second: when the Soviet Union came to an end in 1991, Victoria was not yet ten years old. She graduated from university with a degree in philology in June 2004, just before the Orange Revolution. Now she worked as a columnist and a translator from English; she had also gone back to the university for a second degree in psychology. Ihor, too, freelanced as a journalist, although his degree was in mathematics and he worked for an American IT company. They both spoke English and might have finally given up on Ukraine and settled abroad—had the Maidan not happened.

Ihor and Victoria, notwithstanding their more bohemian aesthetic, were Enlightenment figures much like Pavlo Khazan: they believed in free expression and reasoned dialogue, the public sphere, and the role of civil society. In November 2011, together with some friends, they had opened a small bookstore-gallery called *Chorna Iashchirka*, "Black Lizard." They had no children, they were free, and Black Lizard was a "missionary activity": a space to come together and discuss ideas. They saw how a small intervention like this could mean a lot, how its impact could ripple outwards.

"It's on the street named Red Square," said Victoria.

"Soon that street will have a different name," Tetiana added.

In Soviet-era Dnipropetrovsk there had been no spaces like Black Lizard. Unlike Victoria, Ihor remembered this very well: "In Soviet times the center was completely empty, dark, there were no cafés." This changed quickly after 1991, but to Ihor these quick changes were superficial: they were alterations in appearance, not in mentality.

During the past decade Ihor and Victoria had spent much time thinking about the Orange Revolution, which had been Ihor's second revolution, and Victoria's first.

"We're very much ashamed of 2004," Ihor told me. "I'll explain why. We were among those who happily dispersed from the Maidan with the feeling of a job well done. We didn't understand that the end of events on the Maidan was not the end of the task at hand, it was only the beginning . . . We thought that, having won the elections, we could peacefully go away and concern ourselves with our own affairs and our own jobs, earn money, and someone over there would change the country."

"Good Viktor Yushchenko would do everything for us," added Victoria.

Now they knew: the only ones who could ensure change were themselves.

"So we feel real shame for 2004. That is, we are among those who contributed to the deaths on the Maidan because we went away back then," Ihor said.

And so in 2013 Ihor and Victoria welcomed the chance to pay their debts with a new revolution. They had been waiting for something like the Maidan, something that would truly shake people.

"The events of 26 January," said Victoria, "became that shaking."

The *titushki*, the beatings, the first signs of blood, the random arrests designed to terrorize the city—this was the moment when something changed. This was true even though, unlike in Kiev on 30 November, few people in Dnipropetrovsk went out on the streets the day following the violence. 27 January was very cold, and people were afraid. Ihor had been disappointed.

Victoria had understood that people were afraid, but she had also believed there were ways to break through fear.

"Maybe it's worth doing something flamboyant?" she narrated. "That is, some kind of flamboyant action."

To do *chto-to iarkoe*. Victoria often used this phrase; it meant something vivid, flamboyant, animated. She herself was rather *iarkaia*. She spoke animatedly, vividly. After 26 January, she had had an idea: Ukraine was a patriarchal society; men would not want to attack women. The Sisters' *Sotnia* was a women's demonstration: Victoria and her fellow organizers asked the men to stay to the side while a hundred or so women of all ages carrying pots, pans, buckets, and drums marched to the administration building—that is, precisely where everyone was now afraid to go. The point was not only to break the fear, but also to give people a way to be together.

Victoria was very critical of her own society—the corruption, the cynicism, the passivity; she also believed that this society could change. She saw how moments of extremity like the Maidan forced people to reach out to one another. On the Maidan people's faces became different; bonds emerged among people who had never previously met, connections begun just by looking at others and smiling at them. Once she and Ihor had come to the Maidan in Kiev during freezing rain; it was so slippery that it was nearly impossible to walk, but she had the feeling that she could not fall, that as soon as someone began to slip, hands would materialize to steady that person. This sudden appearance of a feeling of trust changed her, Victoria said. It opened her to other people, made her willing to enter their space in ways she would not have done before.

Mutual trust was also about mutual responsibility, Ihor said. Before the Maidan, if he were pulled over by the police for driving over the speed limit, he would pay the bribe—because it was prohibitively complicated and time-consuming to pay the fine the official way. This was how the system worked: the state bureaucracy did not need to function, because it was understood that everyone paid bribes. This was the only way to get anything done without losing enormous amounts of time and energy grappling with a Kafkaesque system. Yet because the whole system of corruption—Ihor explained—was in fact built on these little bribes, nothing would change until everyone stopped paying them.

Ihor and Victoria agreed that change had been very slow—but they also saw that suddenly, in the year and a half after the Maidan, people around them had changed more than they had in the whole of the post-Soviet period. They had become *active;*

they had reached out to others. It had been difficult to create change when people were atomized.

"We didn't know one another before," Victoria said.

Now in this spacious postindustrial city where alienation from others had been the norm, people had found one another. Ever since the Maidan Ihor and Victoria had been ashamed to pay bribes; now they thought of the people killed on Instytutska Street.

Yet for most people in Dnipropetrovsk, Ihor clarified, the Maidan alone had not been quite enough to effect a shift in consciousness. In Dnipropetrovsk there had been no kidnappings from hospitals, no deaths like in Kiev. For their city the more dramatic break in consciousness came with the loss of Crimea, the war in the Donbas, and the threat that war would come to their own home. Finally it happened: people were shaken out of their cynicism and their apathy.

"We've always said," Ihor told me, "that Ukraine received its independence as a gift, without spilling any blood, without doing anything, and we understood that what's gotten for free is not valued."

"Now, of course, we've paid for everything," added Victoria.

This time, at all costs, they must not squander the chance they had squandered in 2004. In the years after the failed Orange Revolution, Victoria had hoped for a second Maidan—and she was grateful when it came. It was less carnivalesque than the first; in the end it was darker and bloodier—but also more mature. Ukraine had fallen asleep in a swamp of corruption, Ihor described. And he believed that Ukrainians should be truly grateful to Yanukovych: for thanks to his idiocy, they had woken up. As it turned out, they were not fated to remain asleep for ever after.

Free Hugs for Patriots

It was late when we parted from Ihor and Victoria; afterwards Tetiana Portnova walked with me for a long time around the city. Dnipropetrovsk, like Moscow, felt as if it were built on a scale just slightly larger than life. Tetiana was thin and soft-spoken. Like her friend Victoria, she had finished university in the summer of 2004, just before the Orange Revolution. Unlike Victoria, though, Tetiana had remained in academia; she became a social historian of the nineteenth century, writing about the peasantry, the Ukrainian intelligentsia, and the national movement. She taught at the university, where most of her students supported the Maidan—and faulted their professors for their passivity. Tetiana faulted herself as well: she had a young child, now three years old, and so had not been on the streets as she otherwise would have been. She was apologetic for having devoted herself to her baby during a revolution.

Two days later Tetiana came to meet me in the morning with another friend, Anastasiia Tepliakova. This time Tetiana led me away from the city, towards the Dnipro River and a round circus building whose banner advertised "The Illusion of Contemporaneity." We walked past the rotunda to a café on the water. No one else was there.

Anastasiia, still in her twenties, was too young to feel ashamed about the Orange Revolution. She did feel shame, though, at having done so little during the Maidan. When it had all begun, she had been unprepared; she had always thought of Ukraine as a peaceful country where guests were greeted with bread and salt, with borscht and small dumplings called *varenyky*, filled with sour cherries in the summer. She had not been able to imagine a war.

"To be honest," Anastasiia said, "during the Maidan, I was afraid."

Now she was less so. She wore a black t-shirt with Ukrainian national symbols and a large silver cross around her neck. She had auburn hair that was very long; and she was spirited and pretty and sure of herself—in contrast to Tetiana, who was more modest and sensitive to the limits of knowledge and understanding. Everyone was asking historians what would happen now, tomorrow, next year, Tetiana told me, and of course historians had no answers: it was an illusion that we could predict the future on the basis of the past. No one could do that. *"You don't know what will happen now?"* people asked her again and again.

"No one knows."

Anastasiia was more confident, and more categorical. She was certain it was necessary to fight in the Donbas.

"Everyone needs to decide," Anastasiia repeated.

Like in Kharkiv and Odessa, in Dnipropetrovsk in March and April 2014 there had been both pro-Ukrainian and anti-Maidan demonstrations. Anastasiia and her friends painted yellow and blue banners and hung them up around the city, moving as quickly as possible, always prepared to run if attacked. They would hang the banners one day; the anti-Maidan activists would take them down the next. This was at the time when many people, Anastasiia believed, were being pressured to take part in the anti-Maidan gatherings. Her mother worked in a mine, in a town further to the east, where bosses forced their workers to attend the anti-Maidan meetings under threat of not receiving their salaries.

Then Kolomoyskyi came and used his own money to put an end to most of that, Anastasiia added. It took an oligarch on the Ukrainian side to counteract the pressure of the oligarchs on the other side.

It was the war in the east that made Anastasiia into an activist. Victory Day, celebrating the Soviet defeat of Nazi Germany, had always been a major holiday both during and after Soviet times. As Victory Day approached in spring 2014, many in Dnipropetrovsk feared a Russian provocation. Anastasiia and her friends bought first-aid supplies from the pharmacy and spent two days teaching themselves how to apply a tourniquet. That was the beginning. Her more serious engagement began towards the end of that summer, in August, after many people were killed in Ilovaisk, in Donetsk oblast. A Ukrainian soldier she knew there asked her if she could send night vision goggles. So her work as a volunteer began with something very concrete: organizing concerts, collecting donations, using the money to buy night vision goggles, sending them to the east.

There was military gear, and there were hugs, "free hugs for patriots." On the Dnipro River embankment Anastasiia gave hugs to some three hundred people. She gave so many hugs that her arms ached—but she found the exchange of energy fantastic. So there were good moments. Even so, it was not easy to see her friends go off and fight, and to see them changed: leaving as sweet boys, coming back as men who had killed people.

Anastasiia tried to distribute, along with the goggles and the hugs, her own feeling that everything would be okay in the end.

"Sometimes I think that I'm the only one who believes that everything will turn out well," Anastasiia told me. "It's necessary to believe and it's necessary to act. Today, it seems to me, is a time of responsibility for every person, every person concretely.

Every person is responsible for our future. Every one! Every person needs to decide."

Yet everyone was also very tired, and sometimes Anastasiia began to cry for no reason.

Divided Families

My friend Galina, from a small mining town in the Donbas, was in France in April 2014 when her father died. She did not go to the funeral, it was too dangerous. For Galina, Putin was the Hitler of the twenty-first century. Her brother and her elderly mother felt differently. "*We are* the separatists!" they told her. They felt closer to Russia than to Ukraine: Russian language, literature, cooking, ways of thinking were all their own. Moreover, they saw stability in Russia: a strong leader at the head of the state and higher pensions, paid more reliably. Despite the fact that Yanukovych was a child of the Donbas, the years of Ukrainian independence had not treated the mining region well; now they believed that the separatists would represent their interests. They knew that Galina did not agree with them, and so they did not speak about it. Instead Galina would call and ask: "Are you hungry? Are you freezing? Do you have water? Is the post office working—can I send you food?"

When separatists in Donetsk turned Izolyatsia's gallery into a prison, one of its curators, Kateryna Iakovlenko, left for Kiev, while her parents remained in their own town, now part of the Lugansk People's Republic. Kateryna had taken part in the Maidan; she was on the side of an independent Ukraine. Her parents felt differently; when the separatists had taken control, they had chosen to stay. Kateryna's family was not atypical: in the east, youth and education correlated more strongly with a pro-Ukrainian and pro-European orientation than any linguistic variables did. Kateryna and Galina chose tolerance. They remained close to their families—which, Kateryna explained, was not true of many other families she knew, for whom the Maidan and the war in the east had laid bare the divergent values among generations, estranging parents and children.

The war broke up families horizontally as well, estranging brothers, sisters, and cousins, husbands and wives. Many people in Ukraine had close family in Russia; many had themselves lived in Russia; for many Russia and Ukraine had been part of one country for most of their lives.

"It's one thing when Russia is a foreign country," Tetiana pointed out, "and another thing when it's the country where you were born. It's painful."

"I have relatives there, in the Donbas," Anastasiia added, "who say that we're bad people here. It's very difficult."

In the beginning Anastasiia and her family in the Donbas kept in touch, but no longer.

"And what do they want for themselves?" I asked her.

"They want there to be no shooting."

"And do they want to remain in Ukraine?"

"It's all the same to them. They just want there to be no shooting, that's all, and it seems to me that this is the worst possible position: 'I just want it all to be over—I don't care how.'"

For Anastasiia making a decision was a moral imperative. The worst choice was not the choice for Russia or for the separatists; the worst choice was not choosing at all. While she did not want to find out what would happen if separatists were shooting at her own doorstep, she did not believe she would run away.

"And what could you do?" I asked her.

"I'm a good shot."

"You would fight?"

"I think I would. For my own home, yes, I would."

Alchevsk

Valerii and Elena Kozachek, much older than Anastasiia, felt similarly. Valerii told me the story of one young couple in Alchevsk, a town in in Luhansk oblast, named Iurii Aseev and Anna Aseeva. Iurii and Anna, both journalists, were parents of three young children; the father, Iurii, took up arms for the Ukrainian side while the mother, Anna, became the press secretary for Lugansk People's Republic commander Aleksei Mozgovoy. In May 2015 Mozgovoy's car was attacked on the road from Luhansk to Alchevsk, and Anna was killed together with him. Valerii and Elena sent me gruesome photographs.

"All the same she was a good wife and mother," Iurii Aseev posted on his Facebook page after his wife's death.

The story felt very personal to Valerii: he had close family in

Alchevsk. Valerii's aunt had moved there more than half a century earlier, after she had finished school in Dnipropetrovsk.

"She voted for Yanukovych, her children did, too," Valerii said of his aunt and her sons. "When I said that I hadn't voted for Yanukovych, she spit in my direction and called me 'Bandera.' Her son, Sasha, my cousin who's the same age as I am, who spent his childhood with me in our Ukrainian grandfather's garden, considers himself Russian."

Sasha lived with his wife in Alchevsk. He visited often—or used to visit often.

"Our relatives don't believe us," Elena told me. "Take Valerii's cousin, Sasha, who comes to Valerii and says: 'Why did you shoot down the Boeing?' 'Why are you killing children?' 'Why are you eating children?' And I say to him: 'Why did you come here, Sasha? Go back, because we'll eat you. We'll eat you on a shish kebab. Aren't you scared?'"

"Even when he comes to visit us here in Dnipropetrovsk," Valerii said, "the first thing he does is sit down with his laptop and go to the website 'Russian Spring,' then he calls us over to the computer, points to it and says: 'Look what's happening where you are! You've sold out to the Americans!'"

"It's a very common story," Victoria Narizhna had explained, in a calmer tone of voice. "You call your family and they say to you: 'Run away! There are fascists where you are! They've turned you into zombies!'"

Valerii described Sasha's wife as "an ethnic Russian, who's

lived for more than twenty years in Ukraine in a house built by her husband's mother, my aunt, a Ukrainian, and hates everything Ukrainian." Valerii suspected Sasha's wife of actively aiding the separatists in Alchevsk. In contrast, one of Sasha and his wife's daughters lived in Kharkiv, the other in Kiev, and both had taken a pro-Ukrainian position. Their mother tried to bring her grown daughters back to the Lugansk People's Republic. Both refused.

Zombies in the Donbas

Accusations of zombification came from both sides: Ukrainian PR—Tetiana Portnova pointed out—imparted the message that Russians could not think for themselves, that they had been turned into zombies. Russian television, which had a monopoly in the Donbas, imparted the message that Ukraine itself was a phantom state conjured up by the West for use against Russia.

In their 1848 "Communist Manifesto," Karl Marx and Friedrich Engels had described communism as a specter from the future. Now "zombies" emerged from a communism already past. Those in the Donbas who were "absolutely contemporary," Oleg Marchuk told me, had fled, often leaving everything behind. He and Iurii Fomenko believed that all that was modern was on the Ukrainian side.

Iurii, who had gray hair and a twenty-six-year-old son, declared himself by choice on the side of the youth: "Everything that the youth comes up with is good. Everything that those older than thirty-five come up with is the Soviet past."

For people like Pavlo Khazan, the problem was less that people were not thinking up anything new and more that people were not thinking for themselves at all. Pavlo blamed the peculiar efficacy of Russian propaganda. "The level of technology is really very high," he explained.

Yevhenii Monastyrskyi, a graduate student from Luhansk writing his master's thesis about Soviet propaganda in the 1920s, objected to Pavlo's use of the word "propaganda" for the reason that Peter Pomerantsev gave in *Nothing Is True and Everything Is Possible:* propaganda belonged to the pre-postmodern world. It assumed a grand narrative. There no longer was such a thing. Now everything was PR. Reality had become a reality television show.

The power of the reality conjured up on television came not only from its quality, but also from its quantity. Tetiana and Anastasiia tried to explain that the Donbas was a place where people watched a lot of television; in many homes the television was simply on all the time, as a steadying background noise, speaking to one's subconscious.

"People don't believe their eyes," Iurii said. Instead they believed what they saw on Russian television.

After all, as Maksim Gorky wrote in *The Story of a Novel,* "What is reality?"

Pavlo knew that in the Donbas many people believed the stories about the *Banderovtsy;* they believed that Russia would prove their savior, protecting them from the fascists. They believed this "regardless of the fact that Russians are bombing and killing, regardless of the fact that Russia has turned parts of Donetsk and Luhansk oblasts into the Middle Ages, into a territory not only dangerous, but where there could be no civilized society."

Pavlo felt as if he were watching a deformation of human minds not unlike what his grandparents had seen during Nazism and Stalinism. The history of the twentieth century showed that the manipulation of consciousness was entirely too possible: "Germany, the most cultured nation, was able to slide into Nazism . . ."

"We don't want our people dying," said Elena, "because people living in Donetsk have been zombified by Russia."

In separatist-controlled areas of the Donbas, people recreated Soviet pioneer youth organizations and Soviet holidays. Many in the Donbas treated the appearance of the Russian soldiers as the return of the Soviet Union; Serhiy Zhadan described this as "an attempt to revive the Soviet zombie."

Don Siegel's 1956 allegorical film about communism, *Invasion of the Body Snatchers,* and Eugen Ionescu's 1959 allegorical play about fascism, *Rhinoceros,* were both about how individual consciousness could be excised. It was perhaps only a coincidence that while I was in Dnipropetrovsk, a student there wanted to talk to me about the Australian philosopher David Chalmer's theory of zombies. If we could conceive of zombies—the argument went—then philosophical dualism could be proven: that is, we could prove that consciousness was a separate thing, disarticulable from the physical world. The philosophy student believed in zombies.

The Time Is Out of Joint

"The time is out of joint," said Hamlet.

Shakespeare's Hamlet was performed in Lviv in 1943, during the Nazi occupation, at the Opera Theater on the street then called Adolf-Hitler-Ring, in a Ukrainian translation by a Jew whose mother tongue was Polish.

"They're all looking backwards," Iurii Fomenko said of those in the Donbas who were not on his side. Older people remembered Soviet times as an era of security, however relative. Nostalgia for this security was often stronger than a desire for a more ambitious, but more uncertain, future in Europe. Iurii considered this a Russian way of thinking: "In Russia they're all thinking about how good it was under the tsar, they're all looking backwards. They're not especially given to thinking about tomorrow."

"Normal people," he added, "should be thinking about how good it will be tomorrow."

If Ukrainians were looking forwards and Russians backwards, then the Donbas was a special space in-between, a space where time had been suspended. Serhiy Zhadan was born in 1974 in a small town some sixty miles from Luhansk.

"I've always sensed," he wrote to me, "that in the Donbas after 1991 they consciously 'put the brakes on' time, they haven't let time move in a natural way."

The time was out of joint. In the Donbas, separatists were guarding the Lenin monuments; they were guarding the sanctity of the Soviet past. They were also guarding the sanctity of the tsarist past. All of it had gotten mixed together.

Time's being out of joint was not the only reason why Pavlo Khazan and Igor Shchupak related to the Donbas as to a "marginal space." For if the Donbas was not exactly Ukraine, it was not exactly Russia either. Hiroaki Kuromiya, a Japanese historian of Soviet Ukraine, described the Donbas as a "wild steppe," undomesticated fields beckoning as a refuge to members of persecuted religious sects, criminals, fugitives of all kinds; it was a place of "freedom and terror." Hiroaki, upright and polite with immaculate manners, first went there in the 1980s. He bonded with the Donbas, although he was not the slightest bit gangster-like himself. In his 1998 book *Freedom and Terror in the Donbas*, he quoted Leon Trotsky's counsel, "If you're heading to the Donbas, don't forget to bring your political gas mask." Even a political veteran like Trotsky, who had experience with the Reds, the Whites, the anarchists, and everyone else, could not understand what was going on in the Donbas, explained Hiroaki. He added that "'class' and 'nation,' the two major concepts of political thought that arose in reaction to the Enlightenment, did not and do not apply comfortably to Donbas politics."

Pavlo Khazan believed that the character of the Donbas was shaped largely by the social marginality of those who found their way there. Soviet history had played out in such a way that many convicts had been directed to the Donbas, people who had sat in prison, who had survived the camps, who had been excluded from society. The Soviet project aspired to transform these people into "New Men," who could throw time still further out of joint by propelling it violently forward.

That experiment had its origins in one man's impatience. As Marx and Engels conceived it, History moved according to iron laws, and the communist revolution would come about organically: just as capitalism had dialectically superseded feudalism, so would communism dialectically supersede capitalism. The oppressed proletariat would naturally come to "class consciousness": the workers would come to understand that no one problem could be solved without solving them all, and solving them all meant a worldwide workers' revolution overthrowing the bourgeoisie, abolishing private property, and instituting a transitional proletarian dictatorship—until such time as national borders would wither away and all would work according to their ability and receive according to their need. Then we would have arrived at the communist utopia, the reconciliation of all dialectical tensions, the end of History.

This would take a long time, though. It would take generations, and Lenin was impatient. If left on their own, Lenin sensed, the workers were unlikely to arrive at proper class consciousness very soon. What was needed was an elite vanguard of revolutionary intellectuals who could bring class consciousness to the workers, and so speed things along. Leninism meant rushing History. Hence 1917. Stalin, Lenin's successor, held tight to the belief that time could be expedited, and the great socialist homeland could "catch up and overtake" the West. Hence the 1930s.

"Time, forward!" declared the Russian futurist poet Vladimir Mayakovsky.

Under Stalin, the Donbas was the setting for the Stakhanovite movement: superworkers, the ambition to fulfill the Five-Year Plan in four years, the acceleration of time. After World War II, when Soviet Ukraine was expanded to include Lviv, a young poet there, named Józef Nacht, revised the lyrics to the prewar Polish cabaret song "I Made a Date with Her for Nine O'Clock":

I made a date with her for nine o'clock,
for nine—the new time,
She came at nine,
at nine—the old time.

After the Soviet Union collapsed in 1991, something strange happened to time again: it leapt forward in some places, a bit like in Madeleine L'Engel's 1962 science fiction novel *A Wrinkle in Time*, where the characters traveled by "wrinkling time," exploiting Einstein's theory of relativity to bend the space-time continuum. Yet in other parts of the Soviet Union time fell into paralysis. After the Stakhanovite years, the filmmaker Oleksiy Radynski wrote, "time in Donbas went by slower and slower until the clock of progress finally froze for good in the early 1990s, when the state largely shut down the region's factories and mines and sold them off to new private owners for nearly nothing."

Serhiy Zhadan described places like his hometown of Starobilsk as "temporally anomalous zones."

"One has to understand about the Donbas—it's a mountain of Soviet antiquity," Yevhenii Monastyrskyi described the place where he was born. He loved Serhiy Zhadan's novel *Voroshilovgrad*, the Soviet-era name for the city that was now Luhansk, which centers around a gas station in an unnamed place modeled on Starobilsk. "The fact of the matter," says Herman, the narrator, "was that the next place to get gas was seventy kilometers north, and the highway ran through several dubious places, places with no government to speak of, and hardly anyone to govern." Legality in such places was a very vague concept. "Ukrainian law," explained Taras Prochasko during Yanukovych's reign, "is set up in such a way that no one is able to observe it—apart from all other reasons, because the law itself is self-contradictory. For that reason Ukrainian life is based not on law, but on rules. The main rule is that the law can be broken." The lawlessness that was true of Ukraine as a whole was true of the Donbas in particular—only more so.

For its cavalier attitude towards law the Donbas had long paid a high price. Violence was habitus. "The brutality of everyday life in the Donbas astonished metropolitan visitors and other 'respectable' people," described Hiroaki. Stalin took literally the statement by Fyodor Dostoevsky's Ivan Karamazov that if God is dead, then "everything is permitted." This, too, was true throughout the Soviet Union, only in the Donbas still more so.

Pavlo divided those in the Donbas who were not on the Ukrainian side into three groups: those who joined the separatist side for money, killing those whom they were paid to kill; those who truly believed that there had been a fascist coup in Kiev, and that Russia would save them if only they could defend their own locality; and those who were politically indifferent and could not imagine life anywhere else. This last group mattered a lot.

"In general they don't understand that it's possible to leave," Pavlo told me. "A big problem is that many people living in the Donetsk and Luhansk oblasts have never in their lives traveled outside of their own village."

"They've never traveled abroad," Igor Shchupak said. "They've never even been to Kiev. Many have never even been to the capital of their own oblast."

"If a person has only ever seen his own village," continued Pavlo, "his village, the mine, a store, he doesn't understand that life exists. Many of these people do not even understand that the Ukrainian state exists."

For Pavlo the Donbas was a place the Enlightenment had not yet reached. It was premodern, controlled by chieftains. People were used to being ruled by gangsters who collected money from them, Pavlo explained.

"That is, they're used to the fact that there's some—let's say 'person'—who heads the territory . . . a person who represents a mafia group, who has no formal office, who is nobody. He's simply the *smotriashchii*, 'the one who watches.'"

For Pavlo to travel the 120 miles or so to the Donbas was to confront a different civilization. This was a place where the Ukrainian state had failed. The people who lived there "know that there's some kind of *smotriashchii*, there's a director of the factory, or some foreman at the mine. That's it. Everything else is something on television. And so unfortunately, for them—and there are very many such people—it makes no difference what kind of state there is, who rules the territory, whether Russians come or Ukrainians or someone else."

"I have the impression," wrote Serhiy Zhadan following an April 2014 trip to his hometown of Starobilsk, "that most people in the Donbas will accept in a laid-back way the options proposed to them. From Kiev, for example. Or from Moscow.

Or from Brussels. Here it is not commonplace to go out on the streets and influence events."

The history student Yevhenii explained this by way of a story. In April 2014 presidential candidate Petro Poroshenko came to Yevhenii's university in Luhansk; there he promised that if he were to become president, the separatist rebellions would end within three days. That was when Yevhenii began to have the impression that the university rector was changing his party allegiance: once the rector had supported Yanukovych's nemesis Viktor Yushchenko, later he had supported Yanukovych, and now he would support Poroshenko. Yevhenii understood perfectly that this was a political transaction, the kind of political transaction that provided immunity. And he loved the Donbas for its honest simplicity, for the way in which such "transactions" were taken as a fact of life. He described the reigning attitude as this: yes, power exists, authority exists, it serves certain functions, but it is best to keep as far away from it as possible. And if you decline to take part in elections, so much the better: you don't meddle with anyone, no one meddles with you, everything is fine. Because this kind of political adaptation was taken as a given, Yevhenii explained, the parties could change, but life stayed the same. One only needed to remember to switch party banners at the right moment.

"If in western Ukraine people relate to this in a very principled way," Yevhenii told me, in the Donbas people are relaxed, it's all the same to everyone. Of course you can argue, you can talk, you can discuss values, what's important to whom, which party brings what. But on an intuitive level, everyone understands that a party is just a set-up. No one knows a party's statute, and in principle all parties are the same. They're all social democratic, and in reality none of them is social democratic. They're all oligarchic clans.

Olena Stiazhkina, a Russian-language author from Donetsk, wrote about herself: "I would like to be saved by Pushkin. And delivered from sorrows and unrests, also by Pushkin. Pushkin but not Putin." Olena was ethnically Russian and politically Ukrainian. The division in the Donbas, she believed, was a division between the premodern world and the present one. "Nature gives, we take," she wrote, "we do not steal. Who can set limits, if there is no question of ownership? The stronger one. The chieftain. He is the militiaman. If we share with the leader, bring him offerings—the hunt will be successful."

Serhiy Zhadan agreed: this war was not a conflict between ethnicities, but a conflict between temporalities.

In the Donbas the premodern intersected surreally with the postmodern: warlords were using Twitter.

World Order

Pavlo Khazan knew that the borders between Russia and Ukraine were largely arbitrary; for him, though, the point was that international law—the rule of law itself—was at stake. Putin was a continuation of the totalitarianism of the twentieth century. This was a war to excise the remnants of Soviet consciousness, "a war not just for the territory of Ukraine, a war for democratic values."

"And for world order," Igor Shchupak added.

"For order on European territory in particular and for order throughout the world as a whole. For that reason this is a war against the remains of the Soviet Union, the remains of the totalitarian machine."

It was obvious to Pavlo that, regardless of any problems in the European Union, Ukraine should join Europe as quickly as possible. These were questions less about territory than about values. He considered integration into the European Union a necessity.

"I look at the European Union not just as some kind of Euro-zone where the politicians discuss who is more important— France or Britain or Germany," Pavlo said, "but as a system for protecting and preserving our civilization."

Goodbye, Lenin

"'You've knocked down all the monuments, this is vandalism! There's an American flag hanging on the security services building!'" Valerii Kozachek recalled his cousin Sasha's accusations after the war in the Donbas began.

"When I proposed that he drive around Dnipropetrovsk and ascertain for himself that all the monuments—except the Lenin monuments—are intact, and there's no American flag over the building, he just waved his hand."

Except the Lenin monuments.

Lenin died on 21 January 1924. "Death—does not dare!" read the epigraph to Vladimir Maykovsky's requiem "*Komsomol'skaia*":

Lenin—
>*lived,*
Lenin—
>*lives*
Lenin—
>*shall live.*

Ninety years later, Lenin's head was dragged through the streets of Dnipropetrovsk. On the day in February 2014 when Yanukovych fled Ukraine, some ten thousand people in Dnipropetrovsk brought down the Lenin statue. Oleg Marchuk was in his office when he saw the news on the internet. He rushed to the center of the city; when he arrived there were only perhaps five hundred people, but those five hundred were calling their friends, and more were arriving all the time. The historian Oleh Repan was among them.

It was very difficult to figure out how to take down Lenin, Oleh told me honestly. He did not pretend to have had any expertise himself. The dismantling was spontaneous; initially there was no plan, people began to phone friends who had friends who had trucks or cranes or other tools. Iurii Fomenko, who had experience with construction equipment, arrived and advised the others on the technical details of how to remove such a heavy head.

The decapitation was celebratory. Oleh showed me photographs he and his wife, Irina Reva, had taken of their then four-year-old son, just barely taller than the severed head beside him, his hand shyly reaching out to touch Lenin's baldness.

Taking down Lenin in Dnipropetrovsk was part of a larger phenomenon called *Leninopad*, "Leninfall." Hundreds of Lenin statues came down in February 2014 alone. The young historian Volodymyr Sklokin took part in the destruction of Lenin in Kharkiv that September. In Dnipropetrovsk, Oleh and Irina took me to the place where the Lenin statue had once stood. Now the spot was empty; in place of Lenin there was deceptively unthreatening nothingness.

Anastasiia Tepliakova relaxed once Lenin's head was being dragged on the ground.

"I remember very well my feeling," she said. "I'd never thought that it would be physically easier for me to breathe." Yet it was.

For those who took part in the improvised disassembling, to take down Lenin was to leave the past behind.

It was difficult to know where to start—and where to stop. "Decommunization" had caused much confusion in eastern Europe in the 1990s: old monuments came down, new monuments went up; streets, towns, districts, bridges, and schools were renamed; bodies were reburied. This had not happened then in Dnipropetrovsk, where there was still a Lenin Street and a Karl Marx Avenue and where until May 2016 the city bore the name of Ukrainian Bolshevik leader Grigory Petrovsky.

Now statues would come down and streets would be renamed. In May 2015, Petro Poroshenko signed decommunization laws making it a criminal offense to deny "the criminal character of the communist totalitarian regime of 1917–1991 in Ukraine." The laws involved more than purging remainders of communism. It also became a punishable offense to deny the legitimacy of "the struggle for the independence of Ukraine in the twentieth century." This meant the rehabilitation of the Organization of Ukrainian Nationalists and the Ukrainian Insurgent Army, whose members had fought against the Soviets for Ukrainian independence—and had not so infrequently also killed Poles and Jews during the German occupation.

("On the territory of Ukraine, after all, there were also groups of people—and not small groups," conceded Pavlo, "who supported Nazism and fascism. Our society tries somehow to conceal that."

"Ukrainian intellectuals and politicians do not have the right to take the nation's heroes away from them," Mykola Riabchuk argued.

"My God," Anastasiia said, "what difference does it make to us? I also consider the Ukrainian Insurgent Army veterans to be important people, I consider it not right not to recognize them. But that's my personal opinion . . . It's all the same to me if they're recognized or not. We have more important, more immediate problems.")

For Oleg Marchuk and Valerii Kozachek, renaming meant moving time forward. And it was long past time to move time forward.

"I'm in favor of maximal renaming," Oleg Marchuk told me. "Take them all away."

Valerii was appointed to the decommunization commission in Dnipropetrovsk, which was charged with renaming over three hundred streets. For a very long time they had all been living on streets named after the murderers of Ukrainians, Valerii and Elena wrote to me, and now this would finally end. They were unsympathetic to those who found it painful to see the topography of their lives erased.

"It's very difficult for the older generation to accept the changes," wrote Valerii and Elena. "To these people it seems that their history, their lives, are being taken from them. Perhaps that's so, Marci. It will seem strange to you, but we don't feel sorry for these people at all, and we do not even want to understand them."

Nelia Vakhovska, the young translator of German literature, tried to explain. She was an intellectual and lived in Kiev, but she came from a small town about sixty miles away, where her parents still lived and where young people earned pitiable salaries doing heavy unskilled labor at a sawmill where the workers' hands often got caught in the saws. These are the people, Nelia wrote, "who my pure-as-snow friends dubbed the enemies of the revolution." In that little town activists on the side of the Maidan took down the Lenin statue. Nelia learned of this from her parents: "'They tied him by the neck and dragged him

through the city.' This phrase holds unexpected pain." She tried
to explain to her friends from Kiev, and from Western Europe:
"The statue is their personal Lenin, it's where they used to kiss,
where they stole roses from the flower beds, where they went on
pointless parades and equally pointless rallies. Until now, he had
been guarding their memories, storing them all up in one spot."
These are the people, she wrote, who "don't vote in elections, or
if they do, they'll choose the wrong people."

Cicero's Rome

After taking down Lenin in Dnipropetrovsk, Iurii Fomenko and Oleh Repan both went on to fight in the Donbas. Iurii volunteered. Oleh received a draft order. Some twenty years earlier, while a university student, Oleh had taken a course in officer training. The class had met once a week for two years; the focus was on psychological problems in the military. Oleh had never once fired a gun.

"You hadn't forgotten what you'd learned twenty years ago?" I asked him.

"Of course I'd forgotten. I'd forgotten all of it."

Oleh was a historian. His orange-blond hair was longer on top and shorter around the sides. He wore glasses with metal frames; he was thin and bookish; he found nothing at all thrilling about war, and he had not wanted to fight. It was not difficult for him to admit that he had been afraid. Even so, he was a Ukrainian, and he was called upon to defend his country. His wife, Irina Reva, a journalist who was more extroverted than her husband, had also been afraid.

"No woman wants . . ." Irina began.

But she gave her husband the choice: she would support him either way, whether he accepted the order or whether he deserted.

He accepted the order. And she did support him very much, Oleh added. Once Irina even brought their five-year-old son to the Donbas to visit his father.

Irina emanated strength and warmth. Her cheeks were rosy and her eyelashes were long; she was very pretty in an unaffected way, and she was the kind of woman one wanted to have as a sister, or a best friend. On 16 January 2014, she had been among those who danced on the square in Dnipropetrovsk in defiance of the "dictatorship laws," doing precisely what all Ukrainian citizens had just been forbidden to do: gather together.

Oleh spent one month in military training. In April 2014, he fired a gun for the first time in his life; it was a submachine gun. He was very nearsighted, even with glasses, and could shoot only to a little more than one hundred yards.

"Was it hard to shoot for the first time?" I asked him.

"Yes, but that wasn't even the hardest thing."

The hardest thing was being the commander. Oleh had been trained as an officer–social worker, not as a commander of an active duty unit in wartime. Now thirty to forty men served under him, and he was responsible for all of them. Oleh had a doctorate; he was an academic, used to interacting with students and scholars. Now suddenly he was to command a few dozen men, none of whom had higher education, all of whom knew how to shoot. In the beginning it was not easy to find a common language—yet over time they managed, and relations were good. While he and his men had come from very different social worlds, they were now faced together with this one task, and they understood that only by working together could they do it well. Moreover, in a war Oleh no longer differed from them as he did in civilian life; they all lived in the same conditions and slept in the same place. Oleh did not give them orders; he consulted with them and asked for their advice. After all, he had no military experience himself.

And he wanted all of his men to return home alive.

The image of Oleh firing a submachine gun was like the image of the literary critic Ola Hnatiuk smashing bricks on the Maidan—it, too, recalled Hamlet: something was out of joint.

After the month of training, Oleh was sent to Krasnoarmiisk in Donetsk oblast. This was not yet the front; in Krasnoarmiisk there was no fighting, and no one yet knew what the war would be. Some of the local people greeted the Ukrainian army enthusiastically; others were terrified that the soldiers were Ukrainian fascists who had come to kill them.

"People began to come to us very often," Oleh related. "Some of them cried and rejoiced that we had come, some of them were terribly afraid, especially women, and came to ask: 'What did you come to kill us for?'"

Sometimes people came to him in balaclavas. Oleh, though, kept his face exposed and spoke directly to each person.

"'We are the army,'" he told them. "'We are fighting against those who have taken up arms. Peaceful people have nothing to fear.' I said to them again and again, especially the women: '*Look me in the eyes, see what I am saying, look me in the eyes.*'"

Sometimes this helped, though not always—especially given what the people in Krasnoarmiisk had already heard about the Ukrainian army: Russian television had broadcast that in Sloviansk the Ukrainian military had crucified a three-year-old boy. Women rushed to Oleh and told him that they knew for themselves that this was true, that their relatives had told them. Oleh tried to explain to them that this was a lie, that nothing like this had happened, but the women would insist: "No, no, we know for certain."

Yet the longer Oleh and his men stayed in Krasnoarmiisk, the more the local people came to trust them. The area remained calm, and Oleh was very attentive to how he and his soldiers treated civilians. Politeness mattered to him.

"I'm a quite sensitive person," he told me. "I told my soldiers that when we stop a car, we say very politely, 'Good afternoon! Be so kind as to present your documents.' When we've inspected the car, we say 'Thank you! Drive safely. Have a good trip.' So that you perceive yourself as a person and you see the other as a person."

In the end, many of the local people baked *pirozhki* and cooked borscht and brought milk and cheese for the soldiers. When their unit was sent on from Krasnoarmiisk to the front, some civilians cried and asked Oleh and his soldiers not to abandon them. But they had to leave.

From Krasnoarmiisk Oleh's unit went on to Pisky, some three miles from the Donetsk airport. Now they were at war. Most people had fled Pisky; the local shops were closed; and this time instead of the local people's feeding the soldiers, the soldiers fed the remaining people, "as if we were repaying our debts."

Oleh had not wanted this war then, and he did not want it now. He was convinced that if the Russian soldiers from across the border would leave, the war would end at once. He had friends who had been taken prisoner by the other side; he himself had also taken prisoners. Some of those taken captive by Oleh's unit were from the Russian Orthodox Army, which Oleh described as a terrorist organization whose members believed they had come to defend Orthodox Christians and Russian-speakers. In fact many of the soldiers fighting on the Ukrainian side were also Orthodox Christians and Russian-speakers. Oleh himself was not a believer, but one of his soldiers who was spoke to their prisoners from the Russian Orthodox Army: "'Recite the prayers you know.' They knew one prayer, the main one, 'Our Father.' And he says: 'Keep going. Recite some more prayers. If you're

Orthodox, then you know a lot of prayers.' They only knew that one prayer. He recited to them ten prayers—he's religious. And then he asked them: 'So which one of us is Orthodox?'"

In Pisky Oleh grew used to the fear. Worse was the sleeplessness. He never slept more than four hours a night, and often while wearing heavy army boots. Twice during his time in the Donbas Oleh came home for a period of five days, and even then he could not sleep. Irina described how he would shake in his sleep, dreaming of gunfire.

There was fear and sleeplessness, but there was also monotony: at the front there were no books, and having nothing to read became a kind of "exhausting boredom." The library in Pisky had been destroyed by shelling, but where it once had been Oleh found a book about Cicero's Rome. His men would laugh at him, because they would be holding on tightly to their machine guns and Oleh would be sitting next to them reading about ancient Rome. "'Comrade Sergeant Major, what's that you're reading?' There you are, sitting there with a submachine gun, a helmet, a bulletproof vest—and reading that monograph."

In Pisky it was difficult to talk to Irina on the phone. He would wait for a quiet moment to call her; even so, she could often hear the gunfire in the background. During one of their phone calls the other side began to fire at them, and Oleh knew Irina would worry if he hung up abruptly. "And so I say: 'I'm sorry, my darling, volunteers have just arrived and I have to go.'"

"He said to me: 'Everything is okay, everything is fine,'" Irina added. "And then BAM! 'Who was that?'—'It was us.'"

One day after the shooting started in Pisky, Oleh was running towards the front post when there was an explosion. He did not remember what happened next, but when he later woke up he sensed he had been wounded. His men gave him an antishock injection and took him to the doctors, who operated quickly. And he remembered understanding that he was still alive, and that this was the most important thing.

"He called and told me, 'Everything is okay, everything's fine. I'm just a little bit injured.'"

For two days afterwards Oleh remained at the battalion camp, three miles from the front line. Then a friend from Donetsk oblast came and took him back to Dnipropetrovsk. The next five months he spent in the hospital, recovering from a concussion, trying to regain his balance and coordination.

Oleh and Irina's five-year-old son still feared that his father would disappear again.

"After I was wounded, and when I'd come home before those two times, he would ask me: 'Daddy, will you still be here tomorrow?' And later, already some months after I'd been wounded, when I was here recovering, he would ask me every day: 'Daddy, tomorrow will you still be here?'"

Do We Know the Ukrainian Night?

In September 2014 a Ukrainian-Russian filmmaker collective named Babylon'13 released a four-minute video of a man from Donetsk fighting on the side of Ukraine. The man's green eyes matched his camouflage. In the film footage he recited from memory a poem by Vladimir Mayakovsky, his elocution resonant even underneath his balaclava. "Debt to Ukraine," which took its refrain from Nikolai Gogol, laments how little Russians understood of this neighboring land.

Trudno liudei v odno istoloch',
soboi kichis' ne ochen'.
Znaem li my ukrainskuiu noch'?
Net, my ne znaem ukrainskoi nochi.

Do We Know the Ukrainian Night?

It is difficult to grind people into one
Do not presume it can be done
Do we know the Ukrainian night?
No, we do not know the Ukrainian night.

The man in the balaclava who loved Ukraine and Russian poetry was killed during a "cease-fire" shortly after he was filmed.

"We cannot be bought"

In May 2012, Ukraine, as host of the European soccer championship, unveiled the Sergey Prokofiev International Airport in Donetsk. With sparkling glass walls, bright orange check-in counters, and spacious departure lounges, the Donetsk airport was designed to be a hub between Europe and Asia. By October 2014 there remained little besides shattered glass and warped steel. This wreckage remained for many weeks the site of the most savage battle between Ukrainian and combined separatist-Russian forces; the skeleton of the airport became an inferno, a place that was very difficult to get into—or out of—alive.

"The terminals we are holding on to are weaker than the Three Little Pigs' houses," Ukrainian Major Valery Rud told the journalist Sergei Loiko.

In early December 2014 my two-year-old daughter said to me, "I want to watch the Three Little Pigs video."

"I don't want to watch that one," I told her. "I find the wolf too stressful."

"But Mommy," said my four-year-old son, "the wolf is not in our house. The wolf is only in the movie."

Later that month in Kiev I met Ruslan and Zhenia—for whom the wolf was not only in the movie. We met at the Pravyi Sektor headquarters, a claustrophobic office space in a run-down high-rise in Troeshchyna, a working-class neighborhood on the outskirts of Kiev. In narrow corridors young men and women were putting together packages. I had come with Aleksandra Azarkhina, a student from Crimea who, like Kateryna Iakovlenko from Donetsk, had left while her parents had stayed. Now Aleksandra lived in Kiev, and was familiar with the neighborhood. We were taken into a very small room with barely any furniture. Ruslan and Zhenia both had crew cuts; they were not in uniform. Ruslan wore a polo shirt and a thick chain necklace. Zhenia offered us tea in disposable plastic cups that began to melt from the heat of the boiled water. They had just returned from fighting in the Donetsk airport. They would tell not us their last names.

For Ruslan and Zhenia it had all begun very locally. In February 2014 calls had been posted on Facebook and Vkontakte, the Russian-language version of Facebook, for men to gather in their own neighborhoods and form *Samooborona* units against *titushki.* They all knew one another; Ruslan and Zhenia had gone to school together, although Zhenia was younger. They knew that Yanukovych was a gangster.

"You weren't afraid of the *titushki?*" I asked them.

"Why be afraid of them?" Ruslan answered. "We're tough, too." In any case, *titushki* were just guys hired for money, he said, whereas he and Zhenia were fighting for an idea.

They had not been part of Pravyi Sektor then. They had come to Pravyi Sektor only in April, after the Maidan, to fight in the east for their future. They did not want to be pulled back into the Soviet Union. Ruslan, who talked much more than Zhenia did, was emphatic about this.

Putin wants us to be like the former Soviet Union, and we don't want to be like it was in the Soviet Union, which was one big prison, closed off with barbed wire. We don't want to go to the Soviet Union. I grew up in a free country. I grew up with Donald Duck, with Tom and Jerry, with video players and cars and all these things—they're part of my life. I don't want to work from morning to night in a factory, like a slave. That drabness—I don't want to live like that. And he's pulling us back there, he wants to be a dictator. And we, in contrast, are pulling ourselves to Europe, where there's democracy. I don't want to live in the Soviet Union like a slave. Putin saw that we didn't want that, and he decided to take us by force, and so it's happening. If Ukraine loses, we'll be back in the Soviet Union, they'll suck the life out of us, force us to work for next to nothing, push us around. If we win, we'll have democracy, we'll have a future, we and our children, that's how I see it. And they—the separatists—think that Russia is better, they're just next to the border, and Russian propaganda keeps bad-mouthing Kiev, saying there was a junta here, even though a junta is when the military takes power, a military coup. And the military didn't take power here, the people rose up.

Ruslan and Zhenia were honest about their mixed reception in Donetsk: half of the local people were on their side, half were against them—or perhaps it was more like one-third on their side, one-third against, one-third who did not have a side.

Ruslan was thirty-one. He had a wife and a nine-year-old son. When he decided to go to fight, his wife threatened to leave him—but thus far she had not. Zhenia's wife, though, had left Zhenia. He shrugged it off, at least to me and Aleksandra. He was in a man's world now. There were women fighting in Pravyi Sektor, but not in their unit.

Girls made good snipers, Ruslan said.

In his magical realist novel *The UnSimple*, Taras Prochasko had conjured up beautiful sniper heroines who navigated the Carpathian mountains with the grace of gymnasts, leaping from one summit to the next like ballerinas who could fly.

"What does Pravyi Sektor mean to you?" I asked them.

"What it means for me?" Ruslan said. "It's the only structure in Ukraine that's not for money, but truly for Ukraine. Patriots. We will not sell out our homeland, we'll lay down our lives, if necessary . . . Pravyi Sektor—for me—I don't even know how to explain it to you the right way. It's where the truth is. For Ukraine."

"Who counts as a Ukrainian?" I asked. We were speaking in Russian, which was their native language, or one of their native languages.

"All of us who live in Ukraine and have not betrayed our homeland," Ruslan answered. Language did not matter. In any case, it was not Russians but Putin he disliked. He did not want to live under a tyrant.

He was speaking in Russian, Ruslan told us, because his parents had taught him that way. So he spoke Russian, but for him Ukraine was here—he pointed to his chest—in his heart.

"For us Pravyi Sektor is the only structure that has not sold out and will not sell out. We're in it, and we've seen that the people who created Pravyi Sektor, who do everything for it, they can't be bought," Zhenia confirmed.

Ruslan and Zhenia did not trust the Ukrainian army, with whom they were fighting side by side. In the army—they believed—the generals sold out their soldiers for money; the officers betrayed their own men, handed them over to the Russians or the separatists when they paid. In Pravyi Sektor this did not happen.

"With these people," Ruslan told us of Pravyi Sektor, "I'm not afraid to go to war. I wasn't afraid to go to the airport. I wasn't afraid when we were on the Russian border, because I knew that no one would betray me, no one would hand me over. And in the army corruption is thriving, they hold on to their positions and make money off of them, and that young guys are dying—it's all the same to them."

Time after time Ruslan and Zhenia returned to this theme of *prodazhnost'*, corruption, saleability. *The other ones all sell out. We cannot be bought.*

Paweł Pieniążek, a young Polish journalist who had been covering the battle for the Donetsk airport, described *prodazhnost'* as epidemic. No matter how well she spoke English—Victoria Narizhna told me—the ubiquity of corruption was something she just could not explain to foreigners. This was not a question of language; the phenomenon itself was inexplicable to people coming from the West.

Ruslan and Zhenia had gone to the Donetsk airport in September 2014. In their unit of eight men, one had been wounded and three had been killed.

"Was it difficult to shoot someone for the first time?" I asked them.

"No," said Zhenia.

"Not at all," said Ruslan.

They were not used to talking about their experiences, still less about their feelings. Ruslan had a flip-top phone. Zhenia had a smartphone, with Pravyi Sektor's black-and-red logo as wallpaper. On his phone Zhenia showed me photographs: he and Ruslan together with their battalion's twenty-six-year-old commander. Then the body of their commander, his face burned off, unrecognizable. It had taken them thirteen days to find the body.

Theater of the Absurd

"The war is completely unnecessary," Iurii Fomenko told me. "I don't know what they want to prove."

Sergei Loiko, a Russian journalist in his early sixties working for the *Los Angeles Times*, spent four days in the Donetsk airport. A veteran war correspondent, he counted his time in the airport as one of the most extraordinary experiences of his life. "This war is different," he said, "because there were no reasons for it. They are all fictional. They are built on lies, spread by Russian television. There was no reason for people to kill each other. It is a theater of the absurd."

In July 2014, the Polish journalist Paweł Pieniążek was with the very first group of reporters to arrive at the crash site of Malaysia Airlines flight 17, where the remains of 298 people were decomposing in the heat. On 17 July 2014, a Russian surface-to-air missile had shot down the Boeing airliner on its way from Amsterdam to Kuala Lumpur. Those who downed the plane had been confused; they had not understood what they were shooting.

This was a moment when there was much confusion in the Donbas. Paweł wrote of the many people there who went to vote in the May 2014 referendum not understanding the question they were voting on: some believed it was a question about independence, some about annexation to Russia, some about local or regional autonomy within Ukraine. When passing armed men, local residents of a town would ask Paweł, *"Nashi?" "Ours?" "Are they ours?" "Are they are on our side?"* To Paweł it was often unclear what "ours" meant—and he sensed it was unclear to those asking the question as well. Sometimes during actual battles locals would ask Paweł: are the ones who are shooting *nashi? Are they on our side? Nashi?*, seemingly absurd, was actually a very profound question.

Even as Russian involvement in the Donbas became more explicit, it remained unclear what exactly was happening in places like Donetsk and Luhansk and Slovyansk. Who was a Kremlin agent? Who was a mercenary soldier, a paid provocateur? Who had been encouraged with some money to act on his already-existing inclinations? Who was behaving authentically? Who was a federalist, a separatist, an advocate of annexation to Russia? Who wanted to revive the Soviet Union—and who wanted to revive the tsarist empire? Who was a Christian, a communist, a nationalist? Who began as a provocateur but had lost a sense of the script? Who was acting according to a logic whose origins had been forgotten and which now had its own momentum? Who no longer knew who was who, who he was himself, why he did what he did?

"I sense the politics of provocation has led to a crisis of subjectivity in the east," I told Vasyl Cherepanyn, when we met on the Maidan in May 2014.

"Yes," he said ironically, "we are very postmodern."

Dostoevsky's Demons

In September 2014 I was on my way to a classroom to teach Fyodor Dostoevsky's *Demons* to my students at Yale when I got a text message from my Polish friend Sławomir Sierakowski: Vasyl Cherepanyn had just been brutally beaten by right-wing gangsters, most likely a Svoboda youth group. Sławomir included a photograph taken at the hospital: the face of Vasyl, ordinarily strikingly good-looking, now bruised and bloodied.

It was as if the scene had leapt out of *Demons*, as if it had been conjured up by Dostoevsky himself.

It had been the middle of the day, in the center of Kiev. Vasyl, Yustyna Kravchuk, and two of their friends had just left a café on Kontraktova square, near Mohyla Academy, where Vasyl taught. He and Yustyna were walking through the square towards the metro—the same route to and from the university Vasyl had been taking since 1996—when they saw some seven young men coming towards them. All seven were wearing brand-new camouflage; in Kiev camouflage had suddenly come into fashion. One of them shouted, *"Communist!"* *"Separatist!"* The others knocked Vasyl to the ground; they put on masks; and they kicked him in the face with army boots over and over again. Yustyna tried to pull them away, but she was neither very large nor very strong. At one point Vasyl managed to get up and run towards the university. His attackers caught him and thrashed him still more—until a stranger, a woman in her fifties, Vasyl's mother's age, inserted herself between them. This was not what they had all fought for on the Maidan, she insisted.

The police took more than half an hour to arrive, even though the closest police station was only a few minutes away by foot. When the police did arrive, the attackers were still in view; Vasyl pointed to them, but the police did nothing. Before the Maidan, antagonism between the Left and the Right had been a part of Ukrainian street politics. Yustyna had recognized one of the young men from a Svoboda youth group; she gave the police his name. Still the police did nothing—although they knew who this man was: he was known for having tortured captured policemen in City Hall during the Maidan. The police had long been known for laziness, incompetence, and corruption. Yustyna believed that the police did not want to investigate for another reason as well. After all, these right-wing groups were forming volunteer battalions in the east; they were fighting for Ukraine, they were war heroes—so how to convict them for beating up a left-wing activist?

Among the bones Vasyl's attackers had cracked were those responsible for holding up his eye; the surgeons had to operate right away. It was easy to break a nose, the doctors said, more challenging to break a chin, and most difficult of all to break these bones on the side of the face. They must have tried very hard, the doctors told Vasyl.

"At the end of the day this soldier feels sorry"

"These people who are fighting for the separatists, in essence they're losers," Yevhenii Monastyrskyi said.

The reference was to Serhiy Zhadan's novel *Voroshilovgrad*, in which Herman, the thirty-three-year-old protagonist, describes his friends from childhood: "We all wanted to become pilots. The majority of us became losers." Yevhenii knew Herman's generation: unlike Yevhenii, who was born in Luhansk, Yevhenii's brother, older by nine years, was born when the city was still known by the name Voroshilovgrad. As a teenager growing up in the 1990s, Yevhenii's brother had joined a street gang and had been expelled from six schools. Yevhenii knew all his brother's friends: one ended up in prison, another died of drug abuse, "that is, the majority of them became losers."

Yevhenii loved *Voroshilovgrad*. He had spent his whole life in

Luhansk, and much time riding around in buses just like the one Herman gets on early in the novel. He read aloud to me, in Ukrainian, from the novel:

> The windshield was covered top to bottom in Orthodox icon stickers, and all sorts of sacred things dangled and flashed there. These seemed to be the only things keeping the bus from falling apart once and for all. Teddy bears and clay skeletons with broken ribs, necklaces made out of rooster heads and Manchester United pennants had been hung all over the place. Pornographic pictures, portraits of Stalin, and Xeroxed images of Saint Francis were Scotch-taped to the window glass. There were also maps outlining various routes on the dashboard, along with a few issues of *Hustler* that the driver used for swatting flies, and then flashlights, blood stained knives, worm-infested apples, and small wooden icons of the martyrs.

It was a tawdry juxtaposition of images, a grotesquely precise relation to objects that recalled the stories of Bruno Schulz. In *Voroshilovgrad* the visual landscapes were at moments almost "beautiful in their ugliness," as Yevhenii described Serhiy Zhadan's characters. These were the people Yevhenii had grown up among, the people who had inspired his preoccupation with the problem of mass consciousness, his intended topic for his dissertation in the field of Soviet history.

Now, from the point of view of his historical understanding, Yevhenii thought it almost a fortuitous coincidence that he found himself in the middle of a war in his own hometown. That spring of 2014 he experienced what happened "when information stopped coming in, when electricity and water were shut off, when pure survival began. In that moment people really turn into zombies, they lose consciousness." Yevhenii began to observe very intently how people were behaving, where they took their information from, how they processed it. He saw the hunger for news when the usual sources of news disappeared. His grandmother told him that she could get through a day without food, but not without newspapers.

Yevhenii and his father, a political technologist, performed experiments: they would invent a piece of news—for instance, that the Ukrainian army had already arrived in the northern part of the city. Then, while standing in line for two or three hours—to buy bread, for instance—Yevhenii would begin talking to someone, more people would join them, and in the midst of a conversation about trivial, everyday things he would mention the piece of news he and his father had invented, using a phrase they had thought up, including some small details. Then he and his father would study the movement of the information, how a phrase they invented in the morning would return to them by way of neighbors in their courtyard by evening.

"It was a perfect setting for a social experiment," Yevhenii told me.

In June 2014, Yevhenii had planned to attend a summer school at the Center for the Urban History of East-Central Europe in Lviv. He cancelled at the last moment, arguing with his father, who very much wanted him to go. Yevhenii himself was unable to explain why he had insisted on staying: it had just felt important to him to remain in Luhansk.

"I was angry," he said of how he reacted to the separatists that spring. "I wanted to see the earth burn under their feet."

Yevhenii had been on the side of the Maidan from the beginning. He had happened to be in Kiev on 21 November 2013 when his father called from Luhansk to tell him about Yanukovych's last-minute refusal to sign the association agreement. At first Yevhenii did not believe it; then he saw Mustafa Nayyem's message on the internet. It was drizzling; Yevhenii grabbed an umbrella and headed to the Maidan. Afterwards, all winter long, he went to the little Maidan in Luhansk. The following spring when the war began, he uploaded information to a Ukrainian internet site, reporting locations of weapons repositories, snipers, tanks.

"When you've grown up here, and everything is familiar," Yevhenii said, "when you've played on the construction sites—you understand everything and you understand that the city is on your side, that the city is your ally."

On the evening of Friday, 13 June 2014, Yevhenii and two friends were walking home from a café where they had been studying. His bag was full of papers and books—materials for his own studies as a graduate student and for the classes he was teaching at a local high school. It was a very short walk; even so, Yevhenii did not make it home: a few men with Kalashnikovs surrounded him and his friends and forced them into a car. They put Yevhenii in the trunk. He found this very fortunate, because it gave him a few critical minutes to delete everything incriminating from his cellphone: social network accounts, text messages from friends, photographs from the Maidan in Kiev.

It was not a long ride to the regional administration building. Once inside the building, the separatist captors accused the students of being spies for the Ukrainian army. They took away their phones, their watches, all their possessions, making a list of all the confiscated objects—like during the Stalinist era, Yevhenii noticed. Then they put Yevhenii's and his friends' faces to the wall and beat them.

Afterwards the captors separated the students. They made Yevhenii wash the blood from the foyer of the administration building. It was a building he knew well: portraits of those who had served as head of the oblast hung on the foyer's ivory walls. One of those portraits was of Yevhenii's great-grandfather. For Yevhenii this was the most degrading moment: he had always been proud of his great-grandfather's portrait on those walls, and now he was washing blood from the floor in a building occupied by separatists.

His captors kept him alone in an unlit room in the cellar. For Yevhenii this was worse than the beatings, because at least then he had been with his friends. Being shot together with his friends seemed less frightening than being locked away alone.

"When you're left alone in a room and they turn off the light on you, you lose a sense of everything," Yevhenii told me. "That's the most terrifying thing."

He lost his sense of time. It was impossible to know if an hour had passed or several hours or a day or several days.

Yevhenii began to recite poetry. First he reached for, grasped at, the Russian poet Iosif Brodsky's "Pilgrims." The verse was unnervingly rhythmic, a meditation that evoked chills, warmth, shivering. Pilgrims wander the earth, past churches and taverns, graveyards and markets. They wander past grief, past Mecca and Rome. They wander in a world that would ever be a former one, a past world tender and hollow, blindingly snowy, allowing only illusions—and the road—to remain.

("I understand him perfectly," a Polish friend who herself had been a political prisoner in 1968 said to me when I told her this story about Yevhenii. Of course, in such a situation it *had to be that particular poem.* She still remembered her feeling the first time she read "Pilgrims": it was in the 1960s, a classmate had copied it secretly, by hand, and passed it on to her. By then Brodsky had been denounced as "anti-Soviet.")

Then Yevhenii turned to Serhiy Zhadan, in Ukrainian:

—*Zvidky ty, chorna valko, ptashina zhraie?*
—*My, kapelane, meshkantsi mista, iakoho nemaie.*
Pryishly siudy, prynesly pokoru i vtomu.
Peredai svoim, shcho striliaty bil'she nemaie po komu.

—*Where do you come from, black motorcade, flock of birds?*
—*We, chaplain, are dwellers of a city that is not.*

255

We have come here fatigued, resigned, and mute.
Tell your people: there is no one left to shoot.

"It was, of course, such a moment . . ." Yevhenii said to me in Russian when he had finished reciting in Ukrainian.

Yevhenii recited the poetry of Anna Akhmatova and Osip Mandelshtam. In the private library preserved in his memory, he found "Pivdenno-zakhidna zaliznytsia" ("Southwestern railway"), where Zhadan's narrator likened death to a railway conductress: *"for her it is simply honest work."* Later Yevhenii believed that it was Zhadan's *"Choho lishe ne pobachysh na tsykh vokzalakh"*—"What might you not see at these railway stations" —that kept him from losing consciousness.

As in Brodsky's "Pilgrims," in "What might you not see," there was something uncannily rhythmic, a locomotive repetition that moved relentlessly forwards: the coming and going of merchants and jewelers and lawyers and bankers jumping over barricades, the coming and going of astronomers and poets, mothers and bridegrooms, prostitutes and thieves, schoolchildren who are studious, schoolchildren who cannot read.

Zalyshylys' khiba shcho my z toboiu.
Mozhlyvist' myru, iak i mozhlyvist' boiu,
ne pryvid, aby tikaty razom iz iurboiu.
Nabozhni khrystyiany, beznadiini bandyty—
nas tak tiazhko pryspaty i tak tiazhko budyty.
Nam nishcho ne zavadyt' teper odne odnoho vbyty.

At best there is you and I, nothing more
A chance at peace, a chance at war

is no reason to flee with the crowd to the shore.
Pious Christians, hopeless bandits—
so hard to lull us to sleep, so hard for us to wake.
Our lives are now each other's to take.

. . .

Davai, ubyvai mene za nashi spil'ni pechali,
ubyvai za vse, choho nas kolys' navchaly . . .

Come, kill me for our common sorrows,
for all that they once taught us . . .

Yevhenii clung to the words, to the meter and the images:

Doky teplo stoit' nad mistom,
za hudkamy lokomotyviv, za ptashynym svystom,
za holosami bazarnoi nichnoi bidnoty,
doki tut khtos' zalyshaiet'sia, doty
khai budut' vidkrytymy vsi zaliznychni dilianky,
khai diliat'sia khlibom i molokom sonni selianky,
khai bude marshrut lehkym, khai bude riatunok vchasnym.
Rozumu vsim shchaslyvym. Radosti vsim neshchasnym.

as long as warmth hovers over the city
above the whistling of locomotives, the chirping of birds
above the voices of the market's nocturnal destitute
as long as someone remains, so long
may all the stretches of rail remain passable,
may sleepy peasant women deliver milk and bread,
may the route be easy, may the rescue come in time.
Reason to all the happy. Joy to all the unhappy.

The parallelism of the last line, the giving of what was needed
—"Розуму всім щасливим. Радості всім нещасним," "*Reason*

to all the happy. Joy to all the unhappy."—evoked the closing of "Pilgrims": *Udobrit' ee soldatam./Odobrit' ee poetam*, "*Attend to her soldiers./Assent to her poets.*"

"I tried to twirl the poetry in my head," Yevhenii recalled, "so that the imagery would be very crisp. It's complicated to describe, it was a way of holding on to creative thought, it was critical not to lose a sense of reality."

He believed that Iosif Brodsky and Serhiy Zhadan had saved him, that poetry had saved him.

("Yes," a Polish poet friend, himself in his sixties, told me: "when you're twenty-three, poetry can save you.")

Yevhenii's interrogator was a Russian soldier whom the other separatists, locals from Luhansk, called Sasha. About twenty-eight years old, Sasha had a girlfriend at home, and a business selling motorcycles. He had come to Luhansk as a volunteer, he had come all the way from Arkhangelsk, close to the Arctic Circle.

"He related to us with sensuality," Yevhenii said.

And all the others, from the Luhansk region, they related to us like to human material, parts of a crowd. And that was the correct attitude, I would have done the same thing. I know these people, I grew up with them, I've gone through everything with them, and there's no reason for me to relate to them as individualities. I know that they are not individualities, they are simply people of the Donbas.

The Russian Sasha was different.

"He was like a character from a novel. The way he talked about his own life, you could write a novel about him."

"Of course I hated him," Yevhenii added.

The hatred was not mutual. Sasha saw in Yevhenii a university student, and above all, a teacher.

"And here is a very Soviet moment," Yevhenii explained, "when 'teacher' means something elevated, emotional, an honorable person who does very important work: he teaches."

"At the end of the day," Yevhenii believed, Sasha felt sorry for what he and the others had done to this young high school teacher who planned to write his doctorate in history. Sasha wanted to release Yevhenii, but Yevhenii told him he would not leave without his friends. This was a question of honor.

The question of honor belonged to the essence of the Donbas. For all its violence, Yevhenii insisted, "the Donbas is full of joy and mercy—and empathy . . . because the brutality grows out of these principles of honor, from the fact that there is not morality, there is honor. And the brutality, even this brutally understood honor, is for most people in the Donbas responsibility for your own behavior."

In the end the captors released all three students.

"In fact we were lucky," Yevhenii told me, "it was June, and as of yet there was no authority in the republic, only authority in the building."

And Sasha was in favor of letting them go. They had to sign a declaration saying that they held nothing against their captors.

When Yevhenii returned home, he shut the door to his family's apartment and slid down to the floor. His father came in, looked at his son, and asked him what had happened.

He had been taken captive, Yevhenii told him.

His father banged his fist against the wall, walked into another room, sat on the sofa, covered his face with his hands, and cried.

And Yevhenii understood that now it was necessary to act.

Ice Skating Lessons

Like Slava Vakarchuk, the liberal Russian opposition leader Boris Nemtsov was educated as a physicist. During the winter of 2014–2015 Nemtsov had devoted himself to investigating Putin's role in the war in the Donbas, documenting the presence of Russian soldiers whose existence Putin denied. Nemtsov was among those who organized a Russian peace rally against Putin's aggression and the war in Ukraine scheduled for 1 March 2015. Two days before the rally, close to midnight, while walking home with his girlfriend across a bridge just outside of Red Square, the Kremlin on the horizon, Boris Nemtsov was shot to death.

A few weeks later, Slava came to Yale. He was on his way back to Kiev from the United States after Okean Elzy's twentieth anniversary concert tour, and he offered to talk to my students. He was unpretentious, the earnestness in his songs mirrored in the earnestness of his demeanor in a university library.

Boris Nemtsov had taught him how to ice-skate, Slava told me afterwards. It had been winter, they were in the countryside not far from Moscow, Boris was skating on a frozen pond, and Slava admitted that he had never learned how to ice-skate. And so that day Boris taught him. Slava had last seen him the previous summer, 2014, when some fifty thousand people had come to the Odessa stadium for Okean Elzy's concert. Boris Nemstov had come wearing a traditional Ukrainian embroidered shirt called a *vyshyvanka*.

Slava had learned of Boris Nemstov's murder just an hour before he was to perform in New York City. Thousands of people were waiting for him in the Hammerstein Ballroom when Slava came on stage with none of his usual bounce. This was New York, and Slava knew English well, but that evening he spoke in Ukrainian. He had wanted to begin, as was Okean Elzy's tradition, with a song full of wild energy. But tonight he could not. He knew there were many fellow Ukrainians in the room, Ukrainian patriots, and he hoped that they would support him now. Then he spoke Russian—perhaps there were friends from Russia in the audience, too? he asked. He had been close to Boris, he said in Russian, they had spent much time together, and this was very hard for him. He did not want to talk about politics, there was no point in that; now he only wanted this death to bring together all good people. And he was going to begin now with a song dedicated to Boris. He hoped they would understand that it was impossible for him to begin any other way.

Nochi i dni
Zalyshyly svii slid v moikh ochakh
Skazhy meni
Kudy nas zavede tsei dovhyi shliakh
Tsei dovhyi shliakh

Nights and days
Have left their traces in my eyes
Tell me
Where does it lead us, this long path
This long path

Slava was not proud of that concert.

"I was so sad, I couldn't sing," he told me later. He could not stop thinking about Boris.

There Is No Absolute

"The problem is that in this war there is no absolute," Yevhenii told me. "I saw this war, and in some sense I passed through it, and I'm unable to explain it. And moreover, I don't want to explain it, because there are moments of savagery that one simply has to go through."

That autumn of 2014 Yaroslav Hrytsak and his graduate student, Bohdan Solchanyk's friend Mykola Balaban, arranged for Yevhenii to leave separatist-occupied Luhansk and transfer to the Ukrainian Catholic University in Lviv. There Yevhenii met Misha Martynenko, who had recently come from Kiev. Their experiences of "moments of savagery" brought them together.

For both of them it was a time of reevaluations. Misha, a Christian his whole life, was no longer certain he believed. The violence he had experienced in February 2014 "did not contribute to a strengthening of faith in God." He still wore the white beaded cross he had worn then, but now as a memento of those days on the Maidan.

Yevhenii believed that the violence he had experienced gave him insight into history he would never otherwise have gained. In retrospect, he experienced his captivity as a second birth, a time of coming into "absolutely pure consciousness." He emerged with the sense that "I exist only in history and nowhere else."

For both Yevhenii and Misha it was a time of new encounters. Misha's classmate Igor, the antisemite from Svoboda, had continued to fight on the Maidan even after many in his *sotnia* had deserted. During those days in February Igor's leg had been wounded by rubber bullets; for months it was very difficult for him to walk. Even so, Igor joined a volunteer battalion and went on to fight in the Donbas as a mortar gunner. He left Svoboda, abandoned radical nationalism, and became a centrist-conservative. And he grew close to Misha, his former enemy, whom Igor now saw as a young man who had risked his own life to deliver a wounded stranger to the medics across the barricades. For the past two years, on the anniversary of the massacre, Misha and Igor went together to the Maidan to pay respect to the dead.

Misha could no longer remember the face of the wounded man he and his friend Anton had carried.

After February 2014, Misha had health problems: a concussion from the grenade explosion, headaches, nightmares, fear of falling asleep, fear of being alone. For months he dreamt about the blockade, about the policemen with their guns pointed at him. He began to drink a lot. His mother regretted that he had made the choice to fight, but Misha did not. Had he not been there, he would not have had these problems, but he would have had others: he would have had the guilt. Yet he felt no innocence now, either: in forcing open a corridor for the ambulances, in his desire to save as many people as he could, Misha had taken part in violence. And he had experienced the desire to see his enemy dead. Later he understood: the moment he had desired this was in some sense the moment of his own death as well.

Over two years later, Misha, whose very beautiful brown eyes glimmered with a patina of golden wheat, continued to smoke many cigarettes every day. He still held his cigarette not between two fingers, but rather in his fist, as he had done on the Maidan, concealing the light and the smoke.

Everything Is Possible

"Cynicism and mutual mistrust," Ihor Petrovsky told me in Dnipropetrovsk, "—these are the two features that distinguish post-Soviet people." Serhiy Zhadan understood that the problem with *prodazhnost'* was not only that the government was dysfunctional, selfish, and unjust; the problem of *prodazhnost'* was also that in a world where everyone could be bought, there was no trust among people. Trust was something rare and precious, given and received only among close family and friends, not extending to politicians or writers or priests or neighbors. The Maidan was all the more a miracle in such a society; and it was all the more joyous for Ihor's wife, Victoria, to discover that yes, people in her country were capable of something very different.

"Astoundingly, on the Maidan," Misha Martynenko told me, "there were very different people—Ukrainians, Russians, Jews,

Poles, Tatars, Armenians with Azerbaijanis, there were Georgians, Ukrainian-speakers, Russian-speakers, there were neo-Nazis and liberals and anarchists . . . in the moment of danger everyone united and the differences didn't matter to anyone. The main thing is that *you're here*. It's not important who you are, it's important that *you're here*, that you haven't run away."

For Vasyl Cherepanyn, too, the Maidan was precisely *this* miracle. "I am a happy person," Vasyl told me: he had now had an experience of real democracy, an experience that most people never have in their whole lives. And despite having been beaten by right-wing nationalists from Svoboda, Vasyl wanted me to know that when he had been there on the Maidan together with members of Svoboda, he had felt safe with them.

Never in her life had she experienced the emotions she felt during those months of the Maidan, Victoria Narizhna said, "never. That there could at once be such astonishing joy, astonishing sensations, relationships, insights into what—as it turns out—people are capable of." The feeling of solidarity—said Yaroslav Hrytsak—it cannot be described.

One of the men still on the Maidan in late February, unable to go to sleep, told Jurko Prochasko that he would never again be the same person. His friends who had not come there no longer existed for him. He wanted to spend the rest of his life with the people who had been with him on the Maidan.

"The experience of solidarity is central in all of this. Absolutely central," Jurko believed.

There would never be a successful revolution were it not for the feeling that idealism lives not only in me, but also in him, and also in her, and also in her, and so on and so on . . . A wonderful discovery of what a person is capable of. It utterly, utterly changes a person. And afterwards, of course, there returns *Alltäglichkeit* and minor annoyances. Someone bumps into me on the street—"Hey, what are you doing? Look where you're going!" "Look where you're going yourself!" This is the return to normal life. But the experience of people's revealing themselves as possessing such expansive souls—this cannot be replaced by anything else and cannot be bought for any price.

The Maidan was that rare moment of being pushed to the borders of human experience, the kind of human experience through which one could not pass unaltered.

For Jurko selfhood came not merely from thinking. The Cartesian *cogito ergo sum*—"I think, therefore I am"—was inadequate. It was the "I want" that affirmed our selfhood. It was desire that grounded subjectivity. The Maidan was shared desire. For Albert Camus, the desire that led to rebellion was the desire at once to defend an essence of selfhood and to overcome alienation from others. The dialectic of rebellion was that it always began from the individual but transcended the individual. "The sudden appearance of the concept of 'All or Nothing,'" Camus wrote, "demonstrates that rebellion, contrary to current opinion, and though it springs from everything that is most strictly individualistic in man, questions the very idea of the individual." The Maidan was the site of the *Aufhebung* of subjectivity: the highest moment of the achievement of selfhood was simultaneously the overcoming of the individual self, its transcendence into solidarity. The moment when alienation was overcome—when anything was possible—could be as terrifying as it was ecstatic. It was the recognition of a capacity for an authentic encounter with the being of others, when the borders and essence of self were called into question and the boundary between the nihilation of self and fulfillment of self flickered. This state of transcendence was fragile, it could last for but a moment—but it was a moment that most people never experienced in their lifetime. It was an encounter with one's deepest selfhood through an encounter with others, the results of which could not have been foreseen.

Jurko had grown epistemologically modest. He had resigned from the idea that the whole world was translatable, that revolution as a whole could be understood to its depths. He knew that the future could not be foreseen, that the time of myth-making was still to come, that anything could happen.

"Because nothing is guaranteed," said Jurko, "nothing. Perhaps this revolution will turn out just as pitiably as the Orange Revolution—which, as it turned out, was not a revolution at all. But something tells me that this time it will be different."

"It changed my soul," Slava told me.

Dictionary of Translatable and Untranslatable Words

Maidan Nezalezhnosti (Ukr: Майдан Незалежності) Independence Square, the large city square in the center of Kiev renamed in 1991, formerly Square of the October Revolution. The word "maidan" is of Persian origin, meaning a town square or open space.

Nebesna Sotnia (Ukr: Небесна Сотня) Heavenly Hundred, those approximately one hundred people killed during the fighting on the Maidan; from the term *sotnia*, literally "a hundred," in the sixteenth to eighteenth centuries a Cossack military unit; used to refer to a self-defense unit on the Maidan.

Novorossiia (Ru: Новороссия) literally "New Russia," a term used by Putin to refer to (and claim for Russia) an ill-defined region of southern and eastern Ukraine, north of the Black Sea, including the cities of Kharkiv, Odessa, Luhansk, Donetsk, Dnipro (formerly Dnipropetrovsk), Kherson, and Mikolaiv.

prodazhnist', prodazhnost' (Ukr: продажність, Ru: продажность) saleability, corruption.

proizvol, svavillia (Ru: произвол, Ukr: свавилля) arbitrariness, arbitrary will, abuse of power, caprice; associated with tyranny and the absence of the rule of law.

provokatsiia (Ukr: провокація, Ru: провокация,) provocation; a complex political game involving provocateurs often intended to create a pretext for violence.

russkii mir (Ru: русский мир) "the Russian world," the concept of a distinctive Russian civilization to be promoted and protected from the West; associated with imperial expansion.

samoorhanizatsiia, samoorganizatsiia (Ukr: самоорганізація, Ru: самоорганизация) self-organization.

Sem'ia, Sim'ia (Ru: семья, Ukr: сімья) "The Family," referring to the inner circle around president-oligarchs Boris Yeltsin, Viktor Yanukovych, and Vladimir Putin; including not only literal family members, but also closely allied businessmen and politicians.

titushki (Ukr: тітушки, Ru: титушки) hired thugs, rent-a-mobs, paid by the government.

tsinnosti, tsennosti (Ukr: цінності, Ru: ценности) values.

tsivilizatsiia (Ukr: цивілізація, Ru: цивилизация,) civilization.

volonters'kyy rukh, volonterskoe dvizhenie (Ukr: волонтерський рух, Ru: волонтерское движение) volunteer movement.

zelenye chelovechki (Ru: зелёные человечки) "little green men," soldiers of the Russian armed forces, not identifying themselves as such, wearing unmarked camouflage, who occupied the Crimean peninsula in March 2014.

Zhidobandera (Ukr and Ru: Жидобандера) "Yid-Banderite," self-reference of Ukrainian Jews active on the side of an independent Ukrainian state; word formed from "Banderite," a follower of the radical Ukrainian nationalist Stepan Bandera (1909–1959) and *"Zhid,"* a derogatory term for "Jew" that could be translated as "kike" or "Yid." In this phrase, which could also be translated as "Judeo-Banderite," the semantics are transformed from pejorative to affirmative. There is an element of inversion-through-appropriation of Russian propaganda, which imparted to Westerners that the Maidan was fascist, and to Ukrainians that it was Jewish. There is an underlying reference as well to the historical pejorative *Zhidobol'shevizm,* "Judeo-bolshevism," referring to a Jewish-Bolshevik conspiracy.

zombuvannia, zombirovanie (Ukr: зомбування, Ru: зомбирование) zombification.

Notes

Most quotations in this book come from the following interviews; these interviews neither resemble sociological surveys nor draw upon socially scientific representative samples of the Ukrainian population. They belong more to the genre of "conversation," a narrative form that has long played a special role in central Europe. Many began as—and continued afterwards in the form of—correspondences.

Maksim Borysov and Mariya Borysova, Kiev, 17 December 2014.
Vasyl Cherepanyn, Kiev, 19 December 2014.
Taras Dobko, Lviv, 25 April 2014.
Dasha Belka Egorova, correspondence, 23 January 2015.
Elena and Leonid Finberg, Kiev, 18 December 2014.
Iurii Fomenko, Dnipropetrovsk, 30 June 2015.
Ola Hnatiuk, correspondence, 4 February 2014.
Kateryna Iakovlenko, Kiev, 18 December 2014.
Iryna Iaremko, Lviv, 25 April 2014.
Pavlo Khazan, Dnipropetrovsk, 29 June 2015.
Elena and Valerii Kozachek, Dnipropetrovsk, 30 June 2015.
Yustyna Kravchuk, Kiev, 17 December 2014.
Oleg Marchuk, Dnipropetrovsk, 30 June 2015.

Notes

Mykhailo Martynenko, Krasnogruda (Poland), 29–30 July 2016.
Kateryna Mishchenko, Kiev, 18 December 2014.
Yevhenii Monastyrskyi, New Haven, 24 March 2016.
Victoria Narizhna, Dnipropetrovsk, 29 June 2015.
Natalia Neshevets, Kiev, 17 December 2014.
Ihor Petrovsky, Dnipropetrovsk, 29 June 2015.
Tetiana Portnova, Dnipropetrovsk, 1 July 2015.
Jurko Prochasko, Lviv, 24 April 2014.
Markiyan Prochasko, Lviv, 24 April 2014.
Taras Prochasko, Ivano-Frankivsk, 23 November 2014 (audio and correspondence).
Roman and Taras Ratushnyy, Kiev, 17 December 2014.
Oleh Repan and Irina Reva, Dnipropetrovsk, 30 June 2015.
Yuri Riabchuk, Kiev, 18 December 2014.
Ruslan and Zhenia, Kiev, 19 December 2014.
Andriy Shmindiuk, Kiev, 17 December 2014.
Radosław Sikorski, Warsaw/Krasnogruda (by phone), 1 July 2014.
Anastasiia Tepliakova, Dnipropetrovsk, 1 July 2015.
Slava Vakarchuk, New Haven, 12 December 2016.
Serhiy Zhadan, Vienna, 11 July 2016.

For readers who would like to situate the Maidan in a more comprehensive background of Ukrainian history, I can recommend several books in particular. Additional sources are listed by chapter below.

Serhii Plokhy, *The Gates of Europe: A History of Ukraine* (New York: Basic Books, 2015).
Karl Schlögel, *Entscheidung in Kiew: Ukrainische Lektionen* (Munich: Hanser Verlag, 2015).
Timothy Snyder, *Sketches from a Secret War: A Polish Artist's Mission to Liberate Soviet Ukraine* (New Haven: Yale University Press, 2005).
Andrew Wilson, *Ukraine Crisis: What It Means for the West* (New Haven: Yale University Press, 2014).
Serhy Yekelchyk, *The Conflict in Ukraine: What Everyone Needs to Know* (New York: Oxford University Press, 2015).
Serhy Yekelchyk, *Ukraine: Birth of a Modern Nation* (New York: Oxford University Press, 2007).

Notes

Preface

Stanisław Brzozowski, *Pamiętnik*, ed. Ostap Ortwin (Kraków: Drukarnia Narodowa w Krakowie, 1913), 142.

Jean Paul Sartre, "Existentialism Is a Humanism," *Existentialism from Dostoevsky to Sartre*, ed. Walter Kaufmann (New York: Meridian, 1975), 345–369, quotation 367–368.

Ilya Gerasimov, "Ukraine 2014: The First Postcolonial Revolution," *Ab Imperio* 3 (2014): 22–44, quotation 36.

The Sky Turns Black from Smoke

Twitter message: https://twitter.com/olesyazhukovska/status/436436294483591168?lang=en.

The Grandeur of Its Intentions

Albert Camus, *The Rebel*, trans. Anthony Bower (New York: Vintage Books, 1991), 247.

Taras Prochasko, *W gazetach tego nie napiszą*, trans. Renata Rusnak (Wołowiec: Wydawnictwo Czarne, 2014), 28.

"civilizing mission": Larry Wolff, *The Idea of Galicia: History and Fantasy in Habsburg Political Culture* (Stanford: Stanford University Press, 2010).

Mikhail Bulgakov, *White Guard*, trans. Michael Glenny (Brooklyn: Melville House, 2014), 57.

the famine, the Terror, ethnic cleansing: Timothy Snyder, *Bloodlands* (New York: Basic Books, 2010).

Stanyslav Lyudkevych: Ola Hnatiuk, *Odwaga i strach* (Wrocław: Kolegium Europy Wschodniej, 2015), 194.

Fantasies of Galicia

meeting a new person: Bruno Schulz to Maria Kasprowiczowa, Drohobych, 25 January 1934; in Schulz, *Opowiadania, eseje, listy*, ed. Włodzimierz Bolecki (Warsaw: Świat Książki, 2000): 407–408, quotation 408.

artificial palms: Bruno Schulz, "Nawiedzenie," *Opowiadania, eseje, listy*, 15–21, quotation 15.

pharmacy: Bruno Schulz, "Sierpień," *Opowiadania, eseje, listy*, 7–14, quotation 9.

Jurko Prochasko, "Pod wierzchnimi warstwami: Odkrycie malowideł Schulza w Drohobyczu," trans. Agnieszka Sabór, *Tygodnik Powszechny* 17 (29 April 2001).

Jurij Andruchowycz, "Środkowowschodnie rewizje," trans. Lidia Stefanowska, in Jurij Andruchowycz and Andrzej Stasiuk, *Moja Europa* (Wołowiec: Wydawnictwo Czarne, 2007): 7–81, quotations 9, 8, respectively.

Jurko Prochasko, "Europe's Forgotten Fringes," *Europe's Foreign Cultural Relations*, ed. EUNIC, Institut für Auslandsbeziehungen, Robert Bosch Foundation (Stuttgart: ifa, 2011).

The Revolutions That Were Not

Keith Darden, "Blackmail as a Tool of State Domination: Ukraine under Kuchma," *East European Constitutional Review* 10:2–3 (spring/summer 2001): 67–71.

"Likes" Don't Count

On Tymoshenko: Tatiana Zhurzhenko, "Yulia Tymoshenko's Two Bodies," *Eurozine* (25 June 2013).

"'likes' don't count": "*Ладно, давайте серьезно. Вот кто сегодня до полуночи готов выйти на Майдан? Лайки не считаются.*" https:// www.facebook.com/permalink.php?story_fbid=486373798143162 &id=243869855726892.

Mustafa Nayem, "Uprising in Ukraine: How It All Began," *Open Society Foundations* (4 April 2014).

Маркіян Прохасько, "Спонтанний протест," *День* (22 November 2013).

Serhiy Zhadan, *Depeche Mode*, trans. Myroslav Shkandrij (London: Glagoslav Publications, 2013), 4.

Zhadan's Warsaw poetry reading: rbuciak, "Serhij Żadan w Warszawie— spotkanie autorskie," 29 March 2014; http://reportaze.blox.pl/t/42/ Ukraina.html.

"we're worn out": Serhij Zhadan, "Vier Monate Winter" (Warsaw, 25 March 2014), trans. Claudia Dathe, *Euromaidan: Was in der Ukraine auf dem Spiel steht*, ed. Juri Andruchowytsch (Berlin: Suhrkamp, 2014): 63–79, quotation 65.

Notes

Fathers and Sons

Juri Andruchowytsch, "Sieben raue Februartage oder die Rolle des Kontrabass in der Revolution," *Euromaidan*, 7–20.

Jurij Andruchowycz, conversation with Krzysztof Czyżewski, Krasnogruda, 2 August 2014; https://www.youtube.com/watch?v=UOyARyax_Xs.

Taras Prochasko, *W gazetach tego nie napiszą*, 20.

Self-Organization

Vasyl Lozynskyi, "The Maidan after Hours," trans. Ostap Kin and Ali Kinsella, *Prostory*, special issue: Documenting Maidan (December 2013/February 2014): 47.

Andrij Bondar, 12 December 2013, "Diaries and Memoirs of the Maidan," ed. and trans. Timothy Snyder and Tatiana Zhurzhenko, *Eurozine* (27 June 2014).

Sławomir Sierakowski, 7 April 2014, trans. Marysia Blackwood, "Diaries and Memoirs of the Maidan," ed. Timothy Snyder and Tatiana Zhurzhenko, *Eurozine* (27 June 2014).

The Bell Tower

Yuri Andrukhovych, "Open Letter," trans. Vitaly Chernetsky, *New Eastern Europe* (24 January 2014).

Noah's Ark

Natan Khazin interview in Ukrainian/Russian on Espreso.tv, https://www.youtube.com/watch?v=IrACuTpR_ew.

Abbreviated transcription of Natan Khazin's interview in English translation: David E. Fishman, "The Ukrainian Revolution's Unlikely Street-fighting Rabbi," *The Jewish Daily Forward* (18 April 2014).

Jews and the Maidan: Amelia Glaser, "After Yanukovych, Maidan's Next Fight Will Be to Preserve a Ukraine Safe for Minorities," *Tablet* (25 February 2014).

"two of every kind": Yaroslav Hrytsak, "Ignorance Is Power," trans. Anton Svinarenko, *Ab imperio* 3 (2014): 218–228, quotation 222.

Oleksiy Radynski, "Maidan and Beyond, Part I," *e-flux* 55 (May 2014).

Sławomir Sierakowski, "Rosja jest jakaś inna," *Krytyka Polityczna* (11 June 2014).

Gary Shteyngart, "Out of My Mouth Comes Unimpeachable Manly Truth," *New York Times Magazine* (18 February 2015).

Oleksij Radynski, "Czas zająć się kukiełkami," *Krytyka Polityczna* (20 October 2014).

"It was my choice"

Slava Vakarchuk, "The Ukrainian Crisis and Its Future," London School of Economics, 17 November 2014; https://www.youtube.com/watch?v=p m2YCVNMgyQ#t=5427.

Volodymyr Sklokin, 4 April 2014, "Diaries and Memoirs of the Maidan," ed. and trans. Timothy Snyder and Tatiana Zhurzhenko, *Eurozine* (27 June 2014).

When Time Was Smashed

klezmer musician: Interview, anonymous, Kiev, 9 February 2014; transcript provided by Victoria Sereda.

Михайло Мартиненко, "Бои и массовый расстрел 18–20.02.2014 в Киеве глазами студента-историка. Часть 1," *Ukraina Moderna* (26 November 2015).

Taras Prochasko, *W gazetach tego nie napiszą*, quotations 29, 7, 28, 16, respectively.

Yaroslav Hrystak, 5 April 2014, "Diaries and Memoirs of the Maidan," ed. and trans. Timothy Snyder and Tatiana Zhurzhenko, *Eurozine* (27 June 2014).

Kateryna Mishchenko, "Der schwarze Kreis," trans. Lydia Nagel, *Euromaidan*, 21–37, quotations 29, 24.

Aleksandra Azarkhina, "Взаимопомощь в революционном Киеве" [unpublished manuscript].

Automaidan

Kateryna Mishchenko, "Der schwarze Kreis," *Euromaidan*, 33.

Виолетта Киртока, "Киевские суды затягивают процессы над арестованными 'активистами майдана', потому что . . . не могут их найти," *ФАКТЫ* (11 February 2014); http://fakty.ua/176508-kievskie

Notes

-sudy-zatyagivayut-processy-nad-arestovannymi-aktivistami-majdana
-potomu-chto-ne-mogut-ih-najti.

Values

Taras Dobko, "Nauka wolności. Wolności i jej falsyfikaty na poradzieckiej
Ukrainie," *Ethos* 21:1(81) (2008): 38–49, quotations 44, 27.

David Fishman, "The Ukrainian Revolution's Unlikely Street-fighting
Rabbi," *The Jewish Daily Forward* (18 April 2014).

Kateryna Mishchenko, "Der schwarze Kreis," *Euromaidan*, 30.

Oksana Forostyna, "How to Oust a Dictator in 93 Days," *Eurozine* (15 May
2014).

The Very Atmosphere Had Some Qualities

Nelia Vakhovska et al., "Maidan: Collected Pluralities," trans. Ostap Kin
and Ali Kinsella, *Prostory*, special issue: Documenting Maidan (December
2013/February 2014): 6–10, quotation 6–7.

Taras Prochaśko, "Wczoraj będzie wojna," trans. Renata Rusnak, *jestnatu-
ralnie. pl*, 19 February 2014; http://renatarusnak.com/taras-prochasko
-wczoraj-bedzie-wojna-krawa-ukraina/; original: "Вчора буде війна . . ."
in *Галицький Кореспондент*.

Corpses

Serhiy Zhadan, *Woroszyłowgrad*, trans. Michał Petryk (Wołowiec: Wydawnictwo Czarne, 2013), 7. In English: Serhiy Zhadan, *Voroshilovgrad*,
trans. Reilly Costigan-Humes and Isaac Wheeler (Dallas: Deep Vellum
Books, 2016).

Alison Smale, "Lviv, in Western Ukraine, Mourns One of Its Own Killed in
Kiev," *New York Times* (22 February 2014).

The Solidarity of the Shaken

Adam Michnik, "Bracia, podziwiamy Was," *Gazeta Wyborcza* (22 February 2014).

Aleksandra Kovaleva, "Come here and see what real human values are!,"
21 February 2014; https://maidantranslations.com/2014/02/21/alek

sandra-kovaleva-come-here-and-see-what-real-human-values-are/com
ment-page-1/.

Florian Klenk, "Warum die Kids von Kiew wichtiger sind als die brafrackten Burschenschafter," *Der Falter* 5:14 (28 January 2014).

Jan Patočka, "Wars of the Twentieth Century and the Twentieth Century as War," in *Heretical Essays in the Philosophy of History*, trans. Erazim Kohák, ed. James Dodd (Chicago: Open Court, 1996): 119–137.

Hannah Arendt, "Preface: The Gap between Past and Future," *Between Past and Future* (New York: Penguin Books, 2006): 3–15, quotations 4, 6.

Józef Tischner, "Revolution," *The Spirit of Solidarity* (New York: Harper-Collins, 1984), 53.

Grzegorz Sroczyński with Marcin Król, "Byliśmy głupi," *Gazeta Wyborcza* (7 February 2014).

"You will all be dead"

Oleksiy Radynski, "Maidan and Beyond, Part I," *e-flux* 55 (May 2014).

Renata Grochal, "Janukowych zbladł: Sikorski dla 'Gazety Wyborczej' o negocjacach w Kijowie," *Gazeta Wyborcza* (21 February 2014).

Pornographic Portraits

Juri Andruchowytsch, "Sieben raue Februartage oder die Rolle des Kontrabass in der Revolution," *Euromaidan*, 7–20.

Volodymyr Parasiuk: https://www.youtube.com/watch?v=4ysoFDfXQak.

Oleksiy Radynski, "Maidan and Beyond, Part I," *e-flux* 55 (May 2014).

Oleksiy Radynski, "Maidan and Beyond, Part II: The Cacophony of Donbas," *e-flux* 56 (June 2014).

Dialectics of Transparency

Gajo Petrović, "The Philosophical Concept of Revolution," *Praxis: Yugoslav Essays in the Philosophy and Methodology of the Social Sciences*, ed. Mihailo Marković and Gajo Petrović, trans. Joan Coddington, David Rougé, et al. (Dordrecht: D. Reidel Publishing Company, 1979): 151–164, quotation 52.

Jennifer Dickinson, "*Prosymo Maksymal'nyi Perepost!* Tactical and Discursive Uses of Social Media in Ukraine's Euromaidan," *Ab Imperio* 3 (2014): 75–93.

Notes

Russian Tourists

"Ukraine: Vier Autoren im Gespräch," *Frankfurter Allgemeine Zeitung* (7 February 2014).

"Сергей Жадан обратился к харьковчанам," https://www.youtube.com/watch?v=uQMPJFic-48.

Serhij Zhadan, "Vier Monate Winter," *Euromaidan*, 78.

Caligula at the Gates

Tomas Venclova, "Caligula at the Gates," trans. Ellen Hinsey, *The Irish Times* (20 December 2014).

"Open Letter of Ukrainian Jews to Russian Federation President Vladimir Putin," Euro-Asian Jewish Congress, 5 March 2014; http://eajc.org/page32/news43672.html.

Gary Shteyngart, "Out of My Mouth Comes Unimpeachable Manly Truth," *New York Times Magazine* (18 February 2015).

Mirosław Czech, "Rosjanie i Ukraińcy to już nie bracia. 'Umarła we mnie zdolność przebaczania,'" *Gazeta Wyborcza* (6 March 2014).

Slava Vakarchuk, Twitter message, 13 February 2016: "Подивився вдруге фільм 'Майдан.' Думав тільки про одне . . . як воно живеться тим, хто розстрілював беззбройних людей? . . . Що їм сниться по ночам?"

Nothing Is True (The Surrealism of Ostriches)

Yanukovych, BBC interview, 22 June 2015; http://www.bbc.com/news/world-europe-33233716.

Quotation about ostriches: "Что плохого в том, что я поддерживал этих страусов? Они просто жили там, а мне закрыть глаза и просто ходить и ничего не видеть?"

Crimea film: *Крым: Путь на Родину.*

"Full Text of Putin's Speech on Crimea," *The Prague Post* (19 March 2014).

Hannah Arendt, "Truth and Politics," *Between Past and Future* (New York: Penguin Books, 2006): 223–259, quotation 249.

Peter Pomerantsev, *Nothing Is True and Everything Is Possible* (New York: PublicAffairs, 2014).

Oleksiy Radynski, "Maidan and Beyond, Part II: The Cacophony of Donbas," *e-flux* 56 (June 2014).

Notes

Putin's Sirens

Karl Schlögel, *Entscheidung in Kiew: Ukrainische Lektionen* (Munich: Hanser Verlag, 2015), 10.

Fyodor Dostoevsky, *The Brothers Karamazov*, trans. Richard Pevear and Larissa Volokhonsky (New York: Farrar, Straus and Giroux, 1990), 253.

Vasyl Cherepanyn, "'It was a real revolution': An Interview with Vasyl Cherepanyn," *Links International Journal of Socialist Renewal* (9 March 2014).

Jurko Prochasko, "Putins Sirenen," *Süddeutsche Zeitung* (30 September 2015).

Edmund Husserl, "The Vienna Lecture," *The Continental Philosophy Reader*, ed. Richard Kearney and Mara Rainwater (London and New York: Routledge, 1996): 7–14, quotation 14.

Edmund Husserl, *The Crisis of European Sciences and Transcendental Phenomenology* (Evanston: Northwestern University Press, 1970), 10 (translation modified slightly); Edmund Husserl, *Die Krisis der europäischen Wissenschaften und die transzendentale Phänomenologie* (Hamburg: Felix Meiner Verlag, 1996), 8.

"Ode to Joy": 22 March 2014, Odessa; Hobart Earle, conductor; https://www.youtube.com/watch?v=rwBizawuIDw.

The Volunteer Movement

Serhij Zhadan, "Besser keine Illusionen," *Neue Zürcher Zeitung* (6 January 2016).

interview with Arseniy Finberg: Михаил Гольд, "Евреи просто поддержали страну, в которой живут," *Jewish.ru* (27 March 2015).

Divided Families

Mykola Riabchuk, "On the 'Wrong' and 'Right' Ukrainians," *Aspen Review* 3 (2014).

Alchevsk

Алиса Кириленко, Никита Съорщиков, "Боец 'Айдара' о своей супруге: 'Она погибла вместе с Мозгорвым. Бот как режет семьи ета война!'" (24 May 2015); http://kp.ua/incidents/501269-boets-aidara-o-svoei-supruhe-ona

-pohybla-vmeste-s-mozghovym-vot-kak-rezhet-semy-eta-voina; https://
www.facebook.com/freedonbas.ua/photos/a.536519319787551.10737
41826.536398193132997/678658172240331/?type=1&theater (24 May
2015).

The Time Is Out of Joint

Ola Hnatiuk, *Odwaga i strach* (Wrocław: Kolegium Europy Wschodniej,
2015), 385–497 (chapter "Ukraiński Hamlet").

Hiroaki Kuromiya, *Freedom and Terror in the Donbas: A Ukrainian-Russian
Borderland, 1870s–1990s* (Cambridge: Cambridge University Press, 1998),
2–4, 335–336.

Mayakovsky's "time, forward!" ("Вперед, время!"): В. В. Маяковский,
"Баня," *Полное собрание сочинений*: В 13 т. (Москва: Государственное
издательство художественной литературы, 1958). Written 1928–1930.

Oleksiy Radynski, "Maidan and Beyond, Part II: The Cacophony of Donbas,"
e-flux 56 (June 2014).

Józef Nacht, "Umówiłem z nią na dziewiątą," quoted in Ola Hnatiuk, *Odwaga
i strach*, 356.

Serhiy Zhadan, *Voroshilovgrad*, trans. Reilly Costigan-Humes and Isaac
Wheeler (Dallas: Deep Vellum Books, 2016), 36.

Serhij Zhadan, "Ist das wirklich der Bürgerkrieg?" *Frankfurter Allgemeine
Zeitung* (4 May 2015).

Елена Стяжкина, "Прости, Россия, и я прощаю," *ОстроВа* (2 March 2014).

Елена Стяжкина, "Донбасса не существует—здесь будет либо Украина, либо
ничего," *Сегодня* (segodnya.ua) (4 November 2014).

Goodbye, Lenin

On the decommunization laws: Volodymyr Kulyk, "On Shoddy Laws and
Insensitive Critics," *Krytyka* (May 2015); Oxana Shevel, "Decommuni-
zation Laws Need to Be Amended to Conform to European Standards,"
Vox Ukraine (14 May 2015); Volodymyr Yavorsky, "Analysis of the Law on
Prohibiting Communist Symbols," *Kharkiv Human Rights Protection Group*
(3 May 2015).

Mykoła Riabczuk, "Dekomunizacja czy dekolonizacja?," trans. Paweł Laufer,
Kultura Enter; http://kulturaenter.pl/article/artykul-nr-2/.

Nelia Vakhovska, "They've brought down Lenin," trans. Anna Gunin,

Prostory, special issue: Documenting Maidan (December 2013/February 2014): 12–13, quotation 12.

Do We Know the Ukrainian Night?

"My Land," Babylon'13, https://ukrstream.tv/en/videos/my_land# .VRV-PEuvulJ.

"We cannot be bought"

Sergei Loiko, "Ukraine Fighters, Surrounded at Wrecked Airport, Refuse to Give Up," *Los Angeles Times* (28 October 2014).

Taras Prokhasko, "The UnSimple," trans. Uilleam Blacker, *Ukrainian Literature* 2 (2007): 8–57, and 3 (2011): 58–115.

Theater of the Absurd

Christina Berdinskykh, "L.A. Times Correspondent Sergei Loiko: 'What I've seen at Donetsk Airport I haven't seen in any war,'" *Voices of Ukraine* (1 November 2014).

Paweł Pieniążek, *Pozdrowienia z Noworosji* (Warsaw: Krytyka Polityczna, 2015), 113–116, 139–141.

"At the end of the day this soldier feels sorry"

Serhiy Zhadan, *Voroshilovgrad,* 24.

Quotation from "Південно-Західно залізниця" ("Southwestern Railway"): "Смерть, вона як оця провідниця—/для неї це просто чесна робота."

Ice Skating Lessons

Slava Vakarchuk, Hammerstein Ballroom, New York, 27 February 2015; https://www.youtube.com/watch?v=z-H3ZHtROP4.

There Is No Absolute

Михайло Мартиненко, "Бои и массовый расстрел 18–20.02.2014 в Киеве глазами студента-историка. Часть 2," *Ukraina Moderna* (30 November 2015).

Everything Is Possible

Jurko Prochasko on desire: "Everything Is PR: Totalitarianism in a Post-modern Key," 6 October 2015, Kiev; https://www.youtube.com/watch?v=qwMj_WKfEx8

Camus, *The Rebel*, 15, 22.

Acknowledgments

This book would not have come into being had it not been for the serendipity of my presence at the Institut für die Wissenschaften vom Menschen in Vienna during the 2013–2014 academic year, which in turn was made possible by a sabbatical from Yale University. That I found my way to Vienna, and to IWM, is a stroke of good fortune I owe to the departed and much missed Tony Judt and Krzysztof Michalski. My understanding of the Maidan was very much a product of dialogues with friends and colleagues in and passing through Vienna: Harald Binder, Cveta Dmitrova, Slavenka Drakulić, Michael Freund, Dessy Gavrilova, Ludger Hagedorn, Cathrin Kahlweit, Izabela Kalinowska, Ivan Krastev, Kateryna Mishchenko, Klaus Nellen, Martin Pollack, Irina Prokhorova, Mykola Riabchuk, Sławomir Sierakowski, Volodymyr Sklokin, Richard Swartz, Nelia Vakhovska, and Tatiana Zhurzhenko.

That my circle of interlocutors grew continually richer was due to the generosity of many people. Nancy Wingfield, many years ago, introduced me to Harald Binder. Harald Binder and Iryna Matsevko at the Lviv Center for Urban History hosted me in Lviv. The Visual Culture Research Center hosted me in Kiev; Yustyna Kravchuk, Kateryna Mishchenko, and Natalia Neshevets helped me arrange multiple interviews. Igor Shchupak introduced me to Pavlo Khazan and many others in the city now called Dnipro. Oksana Forostyna introduced me to Kateryna Iakovlenko; Andriy Portnov introduced me to his sister; William Schreiber introduced me to Aleksandra Azarkhina, and to Iuliia Mendel, who arranged the interview with Ruslan and Zhenia; Harald Binder introduced me to Ostap and Victoria Sereda. Ostap and Victoria kept me company in Lviv—and introduced me to Iryna Iaremko. Yaroslav Hrytsak shared his students with me. Martin Pollack introduced me to Jurko Prochasko. Martin also, if less directly, introduced me to Serhiy Zhadan: in Vienna, on the evening of 4 March 2014, Martin opened his presentation of the German translation of my book *The Taste of Ashes* by reading a fragment of one of Serhiy Zhadan's novels in German translation. This was part of a decision made that winter by German and Austrian writers to begin every literary event by reading a short text by a Ukrainian author. That evening took place just three days after Serhiy was beaten in demonstrations in Kharkiv; it was unclear then whether or not he would recover.

My gratitude to all of the people who appear in this book goes without saying; it is not easy to open oneself to a historian's voyeurism. Yet the precondition for empathy is precisely such voyeurism and such generosity; that I was able to write this book and tell these stories is only because the protagonists chose to trust me, and to make themselves vulnerable.

Jurko Prochasko told me that he had abandoned the idea that the whole world was *übersetzbar*—that is, translatable. Nonetheless, writing history is an act of faith that at least *something* can be translated, that some kind of understanding of others is possible. This was a project that involved five different languages and an enormous amount of translation. And I was privileged to be working with people who understood the weight of language and the responsibility writers take for each word. Karolina Jesień transcribed a very long interview with Jurko Prochasko in Polish; Aleksandra Azarkhina transcribed all of the Russian-language interviews. That I was able (I think and I hope) to be very precise in my translations into English was made possible by Karolina's and Aleksandra's careful Polish and Russian (and occasionally Ukrainian) transcriptions from the audio recordings. Volodymyr Kulyk and Kate Younger patiently corrected my transliterations from Ukrainian; Amelia Glaser, Volodymyr Kulyk, and Timothy Snyder worked with me on the translations of Serhiy Zhadan's poetry; Amelia and Alexander Zeyliger have long been my regular interlocutors when I translate from Russian. (I have been exploiting Sasha's literary translation talents for the better part of twenty years, and I can no longer even imagine thinking about either Eastern Europe or literature without Amelia.) I take responsibility for any and all imperfections.

The "Ukraine: Thinking Together" conference held in May 2014 in Kiev was something remarkable. The gathering was originally the idea of Leon Wieseltier and Franklin Foer; Oksana Forostyna, Timothy Snyder, Kate Younger, and Tatiana Zhurzhenko made it happen. I owe special thanks as well to the journalists and editors at *Gazeta Wyborcza* for their fantastic live-feed coverage of the Maidan in February 2014; to Mari Bastashevski and Martha Bojko for conversations in New Haven; to Masha Gessen for conversations in New York, Kiev, and Vienna about totalitarianisms past and present; to Sławomir Sierakowski and Michał Sutowski for always wanting me to write; to Lynne Viola for an exceptional seminar in Soviet history, which I have never forgotten; to Hiroaki Kuromiya and Norman Naimark for being models of impeccable integrity as historians; and to Alexander Prusin for imparting understandings to me about the Soviet project in general and Ukraine in particular that I have still not yet fully put into words, all these years later. The S. Fischer Stiftung invited me to Russia; Peter Schwarz arranged the trip despite the difficulty of acquiring the visa. It felt especially important to me to go back to Russia before I finished this book, and I am indebted to Peter, the Fischer Stiftung, and all of the organizers of the "Debates on Europe" for bringing me there. That my Russian could be resurrected after all these years owes everything to the unusually firm foundation Todd Armstrong, Yuliya Morozova, and Lyudmila Parts gave me in Middlebury nearly two decades ago. Frank Berberich, editor of *Lettre International,* published with great care—and indulgence for its length—my essay about Jurko Prochasko, "Entscheidung am Majdan: Eine Phänomenologie der Ukrainischen Revolution," which later developed into this book. Bernhard Schmid did an excellent job with the English translation; Martin Pollack—while riding on a train through the Ukrainian provinces—translated the Polish citations directly into German.

Steve Wasserman read the original essay published in *Lettre International* and believed it should be a book. Gillian MacKenzie, my literary agent, and Vanessa Mobley, the editor of *The Taste of Ashes,* believed that I could write this book from the very beginning—much sooner than I believed it myself. Steve and Jaya Aninda Chatterjee at Yale University Press carefully guided the book through production; Jeffrey Schier copyedited the manuscript with much sensitivity and attentiveness.

This book manuscript had many perceptive readers in earlier drafts: my undergraduate and graduate students in various seminars at Yale; Aaron Sachs's "Historians Are Writers" workshop at Cornell University; the Russian and East European Reading Group at the University of California at San Diego; Krytyka Polityczna in Warsaw; the participants of the workshop "Reading the Other: Tony Judt reads Hannah Arendt, Albert Camus, Czesław Miłosz, and Leszek Kołakowski" at the Borderlands Foundation in Krasnogruda; and Mykola Balaban, Holly Case, Krzysztof Czyżewski, Leonidas Donskis, Slavenka Drakulić, Olenka Dzhedzhora, Carl Henrik Fredriksson, Amelia Glaser, Irena Grudzinska-Gross, Hans Ulrich Gumbrecht, Yaroslav Hrytsak, Izabela Kalinowska, Volodymyr Kulyk, Hiroaki Kuromiya, Gillian Mackenzie, Yevhenii Monastyrskyi, Norman Naimark, Andriy Portnov, Dan Shore, Timothy Snyder, Stephanie Steiker, Elli Stern, Marcin Szuster, Steve Wasserman, and Larry Wolff.

It was the Ukrainian revolution that prompted me to leave both my small children overnight for the first time and go to Ukraine on my own. I owe an entirely different level of gratitude to Melanie Angerler, Izabela Kalinowska, Elena Peretschesova, and Salamat Sungurova for taking such good care of them while I was away. Almost all of the substantive writing of this book took place over three summers in Krasnogruda, a very special place for thinking and for writing. In Krasnogruda my family and I were warmly received by Krzysztof Czyżewski and Małgorzata Sporek-Czyżewska and Marek Pawlowski (who knows how to do everything). Olga Goździewska, Iwona Milewska, and Dominika Zawadzka—"*nasze dziewczyny*"—ran around in the woods every day with my children, constructing rustic cafés for *ślimaki,* feeding stray hedgehogs, and cultivating their friendship with Rumi, the dachshund lord of Czesław Miłosz's manor, and Grażenka, his more docile French bulldog companion. This is what made it possible for their mother (and father) to write. Krzysztof was the ideal interlocutor, ever gentle yet ever incisive, for several public conversations in the very beautiful café *Piosenka o porcelanie*, before a very gratifying audience who appeared, literally, from out of the forest.

My friend Lida Havriljukova introduced me to Ukraine—and the Donbas —all those years ago in yet another country about which we know little. In some sense this book grows out of an unexpected encounter between two foreign women living in a small Czech town in the mid-1990s.

Alitta Dercaci and Shakila McKnight took exceptionally good care of Kalev and Talia in New Haven while I was finishing this book. Slava Vakarchuk, with much affection and patience for small children, gave Kalev and Talia bouncing lessons after they watched a video of Okean Elzy's concert in Kiev and decided they wanted to learn to "bounce like a bunny" like Slava. He also invited them to their first-ever rock concert—and opened, at Talia's request, with "Slava's wake-up song." Kalev and Talia learned *"Vstavai!"* from Slava, and the "Ode to Joy" of Beethoven's Ninth Symphony from the video Ola Hnatiuk sent to me of the flash mob orchestra at the Odessa market. Timothy Snyder understood why it all mattered.